Advance Praise

Animal Mayhem bursts with heart—stories that made me laugh, tear up, and fall in love with every creature on the page. These tales capture the hilarious, tender chaos of life with animals, from skunks to starter pets and everything in between. Each chapter honors the wild, unpredictable joy our furry and feathered companions bring to our lives. There truly is something here for every animal lover. I highly recommend this delightful collection.

—Jill Celeste, MA, author, *Loud Woman: Goodbye, Inner Good Girl!*

Animal Mayhem: When Wild Things Go Wilder will bend you in half with laughter and send you running to hug your furry family members. This is a must-have book because everyone loves heartfelt and fun-filled animal stories.

— Stacey Wilk, best-selling and award-winning author of *Sea Glass Wrapped in Red*

If you've ever been owned by a pet—especially one that's redecorated your house in the most dramatic ways—this book is for you! Revel in this newest dose of *Animal Mayhem* for smiles, belly laughs, and reminders of the beautiful absurdity of life, and how even the biggest "oh no!" moments can turn out exactly right.

— **Kris Faatz, award-winning author of *Fourteen Stones* and *Line Magic***

This collection is a masterclass in the "messy-beautiful" reality of pet ownership! I was laughing out loud at the "skunk secret" a wife kept from her husband, but my heart absolutely overflowed reading about Jackson—the "farm hooligan" dog who proved that being ready is better than being perfect and helped a family finally find their way to their son. It's a stunning reminder that sometimes the most chaotic animal mayhem is exactly what we need to lead us home.

— **Summer Nitsch, founder of Superior Effect Marketing**

So many unique animal stories, especially one about a quirky adopted skunk-loving dog helping a family make their human adoption dreams come true—an excellent read for book and animal enthusiasts of all ages.

— **Charleen Balcer, student**

Who knew the chupacabra is far more terrifying than folklore ... it could be lurking in your dear friend's home, wreaking havoc on their family!

— **Kelly Newcomb-Hoehn, animal lover and ardent reader**

Animal Mayhem: When Wild Things Go Wilder effectively conveys how the animals in our world can be mischievous and unpredictable while also heartwarming, endearing, and a source of loving companionship. If you want a feel-good reading experience, this anthology offers just that.

— **Kim Fasula, reader and golden retriever lover**

Loved this! The stories were funny and entertaining; they kept one's interest going. A great collection of stories to enjoy while sitting by a fire, while sipping on hot chocolate.

— **Linda Letourneau**

Animal Mayhem

Also in the Burnt Gloveboxes Series

Burnt Gloveboxes (*Vol. II*) by Gina Ramsey

Burnt Gloveboxes (*Vol. I*) by Gina Ramsey

Animal Mayhem

When Wild Things Go Wilder

Burnt Gloveboxes III

Foreword by
Professor Frank Chindamo, CHP

Highlander Press does not condone or endorse animal abuse of any kind. The stories within this anthology reflect the lived experiences, perspectives, and memories of the contributors. Some narratives may depict difficult circumstances involving animals; these elements are included solely to honor each writer's authentic experience.

ISBN: 978-1-956442-67-0
ebook ISBN: 978-1-956442-68-7
Library of Congress Control Number: Applied for

Published by Highlander Press
501 W. University Pkwy, Suite B-2
Baltimore, MD 21210

Cover design: Patricia Creedon (www.patcreedondesigns.com)
Editor: Deborah Kevin, MA (www.deborahkevin.com)
Author photo: JoAnn Jardine, Studio One Photography

Contents

This book is dedicated to all the furry friends who have brought many years of love, joy, and laughter to my life, including my Piper. You will always be Grandma's girl.

Foreword

Professor Frank Chindamo, CHP

Gina asked me to write the foreword for this book. I said, "Sure, I can write four words." In fact, that was six words right there!

"No," she said. "A *foreword*."

So I panicked.

How does one write a foreword for a book? I don't even *read* forewords. And besides—you, dear reader, don't know me. Why would you read something I wrote?

There could be only one explanation: You like to read. That alone makes you a bit of a unicorn these days. Refreshing.

And if you like to read, then you probably have a functioning brain. Which is exactly why you picked up this book. While others are slouched over their phones, consuming endless AI slop—artificial dolphins playing artificial pianos, monkey conductors on lollipop trains, and other bizarre digital nonsense—you're here, choosing something real.

Bravo. Gold star. Yay, you.

And you're in luck, because this book *is* real.

The stories are real. The writers are real. The animals are real. And the love, chaos, laughter, and meaning woven through these pages? Very real. I smiled. I laughed. I even let out a few spontaneous "Awwwws."

So please—read on, dear reader. Stop wasting time on AI nonsense. Sure, the video of the bullfighting chihuahua *looks* real, but it's not. We already have more than enough fake in our lives.

This book is the real deal. The good stuff. The bee's knees—*actual* knees, not AI-generated ones.

So get to it. Really. Why are you still here?

The animals and their humans are far more lovable than this foreword. You'll fall for every pet, every owner, and every heartwarming, hilarious story inside.

Seriously ... still here?

Move along already.

Introduction

Gina Ramsey

My husband, Paul, and I donned our thickest winter coats, grabbed mittens and hand warmers, and headed for the door. I snatched up two chicken thigh skins left over from dinner and shoved them into a quart-sized Ziploc baggie. For good measure, I added a handful of dog biscuits.

We shuffled onto the side porch, and it felt as if frozen daggers struck my face. The temperature had plunged to a dangerous twenty degrees below zero.

Just thirty minutes earlier, I had read a cry for help on Facebook: *Missing dog. Goldendoodle. Murphy. Village of 63rd and Oaks. Anyone seen him?*

Worried the dog would freeze to death if he wasn't found quickly, we braved the brutal cold and joined the neighborhood goldendoodle search-and-rescue team.

As we stepped to the edge of the deck, Paul suddenly said, "Look over there!" His oversized mitten pointed toward the house kitty-corner from ours.

There he was—Murphy, the rogue goldendoodle—standing tall in the front yard. A streetlight illuminated him like a Hollywood spotlight. I couldn't believe it. We had found him immediately. **SCORE!**

At the same time, we both tried coaxing him with enthusiastic calls of, "Hey, Murphy! Come here, boy!"

Unfortunately, "come here" translated to *it's go time.* Murphy bolted southbound, and the chase was on.

"Let's go! Get in the truck!" Paul yelled. Clouds of steam puffed from our mouths as we waddled like giant penguins down the icy steps and across the driveway. We piled into the official chase vehicle, rounded the corner—and Murphy was gone.

Moments later, we spotted him trotting down the middle of the next street. We followed slowly. He glanced back, darted left, and disappeared between houses toward an alley. Gone again.

"He's just like Rusty," Paul said.

He was right. Years earlier, we had gained plenty of experience chasing Rusty, our golden retriever, who routinely escaped and tore through the neighborhood like a furry fugitive.

Like Rusty, Murphy had perfected the art of slipping between houses to avoid capture. After several near misses, we finally found Murphy sitting on someone's side porch.

"There he is! Get out!" Paul said.

Clutching my baggie of chicken skin and biscuits, I jumped out of the truck and cautiously approached. The chase through the bitter cold had clearly tired Murphy out. I pulled out the chicken skin and inched closer, hoping he was finally out of steam.

"Hey, Murphy. Hey, buddy. Look what I have for you." I climbed the porch steps slowly, hoping to get close enough to grab his collar. He looked at the chicken skin, then at me—and instantly figured out my plan. Murphy sprang up, bounded down the steps, and skittered into the front yard. I followed, pleading, "No, no ... it's okay, boy. Murphy, stay ... Murphy, SIT!"

To my surprise, he plopped his butt down in the snow.

"Good boy," I said. I crouched again and offered the chicken skin. Still no interest. Clearly, he didn't trust my cooking—and I couldn't blame him. I dropped the chicken skin onto the snow and reached for a biscuit instead.

That's when the pain hit. My fingers throbbed and burned. In the rush, I had left my gloves in the truck—an unwise decision in frostbite territory. "Want a treat? Want a biscuit, Murphy?" I asked.

Suspicion flickered between Murphy and the biscuit. Just then, a white truck pulled up to the curb. A slender man stepped out and approached cautiously. Murphy stood, tense, ready to bolt again.

"Murphy, SIT!" I ordered. Once again, he plopped down and watched the man.

It was Murphy's owner. The man took slow, careful steps forward. "Murphy," he said gently. "Come on, Murph. It's okay. Let's go home."

Murphy stood and calmly walked into his owner's arms. The man looked at me, sheepish and relieved. "Thank you," he said.

They loaded into the truck and disappeared into the darkness.

Back in our truck, I pressed my frozen fingers against the heat vents and took a deep breath, relieved that this fur baby would soon be warm and safe at home.

On the drive back, Paul and I laughed about Rusty and the chaos he had created each time he escaped.

That night, as I lay my head on the pillow, a thought popped into my head. *That dog. His name was Murphy.* I giggled at the irony.

Murphy's Law—the idea that *anything that can go wrong, will go wrong*—had inspired my previous books, *Burnt Gloveboxes* Volumes I and II. Now, here was an actual Murphy creating mayhem just as my animal mishaps anthology was about to be published.

Coincidence? I'll let you decide.

My motto had always been to find the funny—or at least the positive—in life's mishaps, and this one fit perfectly. A Murphy's Law moment starring a dog named Murphy felt like the universe winking at me.

Animals—whether household pets, farm friends, or wildlife—had always held a special place in my heart. They brought joy, chaos, and unexpected harmony into our lives. On bad days, pets somehow sensed our moods and curled up beside us, silently assuring us that everything would be okay. Other times, they launched into wild zoomies that left us laughing despite ourselves.

Sometimes, that joy came from falling down a social media rabbit hole—watching donkeys play with rubber chickens, gorillas react in astonishment to magic tricks, or raccoons redecorate yards with someone else's trash.

Whether fur, feathers, fins, scales, or tails, shenanigans were inevitable. Animals were often the drivers of the crazy bus, happily taking us humans along for the ride. *Animal Mayhem* is chock-full of wild, witty, and wacky animal hijinks. I hope these stories will spark laughter, bring joy, and maybe even help readers feel a little less alone in their own animal mishaps.

Welcome to *Animal Mayhem: When Wild Things Go Wilder*!

How a Dog Named Jackson Helped Us Become a Family

Jen Kline Clark

In 2007, after three long years of infertility—multiple pregnancies that didn't make it, endless doctor visits, and heartbreak after heartbreak—my husband Patrick and I were emotionally wrecked. Eventually, one doctor looked me in the eye and gently said, "This isn't the path. It's time to look elsewhere."

So, we did. That January, we began the adoption process.

If you've ever adopted, you know it's no small thing. There's paperwork. There are interviews. There's more paperwork. And then—once you've been thoroughly approved as human beings—you have to pass a *home study*, where a social worker comes into your home to assess if you're suitable parents.

But here's the kicker: Once the home study is complete, you get to tell your story—on just one double-sided sheet of paper. That page is what the expectant birth mom sees when she's choosing who will raise her child. One page. Front and back. Your whole heart. Your whole story.

And I had a picture in my head of exactly what ours needed to be: us ... and a dog.

Our sweet pup had passed away shortly before the home study, but I *knew* that dog had to be part of our story. I believed—down to my toes—that a birth mom would see that photo and feel something in her heart. But we didn't have a dog. And time was ticking.

So, my mom called my aunt Dawn in Virginia, who raised golden retrievers on her big, wild chicken farm. She didn't have any puppies at the time—but, as fate would have it, she *did* have one dog in need of a home.

Jackson.

He'd been adopted once but was quickly returned when his owner turned out to be severely allergic. Because of that, his papers were no longer "clean," so he couldn't be placed with new buyers. He'd been living on the farm for months, running wild, getting into trouble with the breeding dogs, and generally acting like a lovable farm hooligan.

Aunt Dawn adored him—but it was clear he needed a different kind of home. And we were on a deadline.

We drove down to Virginia the next day, met Jackson, and brought him home. He was a beautiful golden, barely two years old, raised in total freedom—no leashes, no structured bathroom habits. He'd grown up with swinging farm doors and self-regulated potty breaks. You can imagine his confusion when we handed him a collar and a leash and said, "Welcome to suburbia."

He didn't like the collar. Hated the leash. Could not fathom why we insisted on accompanying him outside every few hours to do his business.

But we worked on it. Slowly. Lovingly. Leading up to the home study, we had Jackson on a solid potty-training schedule—walks every couple of hours, even in the middle of the night.

Which brings us to the night before the social worker arrived.

The house was spotless. Like, *sparkling*. I'd bleached everything. Patrick was tense. I was jittery. Jackson was ... Jackson.

At 4:00 a.m., our alarm went off for his early morning walk. Patrick dragged himself out of bed, clipped on the leash, and stepped out into the thick, humid August air. They walked the edge of our yard near a drainage ditch between our house and the neighbor's. At the end of the ditch? A big, dark storm pipe.

Jackson dove in.

No warning. Just launched himself into that pipe—and immediately got sprayed by a skunk. Right in the face. In the mouth. All along one side of his body.

Patrick ran to the front door for help. Tried to stay outside to yell for me, but a glob of skunk goo dropped on the floor by the entryway. And that's when the stench hit.

Skunk stench is not like regular stench. It *bombs* the air. One drop in your house and it's like a skunk dropped a stink grenade. The stinks crawled into every crevice. Even your drawers would held the smell to surprise you weeks later.

I came racing down the stairs. We had no time to panic—we had to act. I googled the fastest de-skunk home concoction I could find: baking soda, Dawn dish soap, hydrogen peroxide. Mixed into a paste. I slathered Jackson in it outside while Patrick held the leash. Then we rinsed him with the hose.

Jackson—farm-raised, freedom-loving Jackson—hated the hose with a fiery passion. In one slippery, panicked move, he slipped out of his too-loose collar (a farm leftover) and bolted.

He ran around the yard. He ran around *us*. Then—of course—he ran straight through the open front door into the house, right up onto our clean couch, and began furiously rubbing his gooey, skunky body all over the cushions.

We wrestled him back outside, found a smaller collar, and did our best to clean him properly. But it was too late. We had a wet, frustrated, not the least bit de-skunked dog. A house that reeked. A couch that was basically a stink sponge was moved outside, lining our garage. And a social worker was due in three hours.

We threw Jackson in the garage, bleached everything we could, turned on every fan, opened every window, and just ... waited.

At 9:00 a.m. sharp, she pulled into the driveway.

I met her at the door, all but blurting, "I have a story for you." I offered to give her a quick tour and then take her out for breakfast—far, far away from the stench. She didn't even blink.

"Nope," she said. "This is a home study. We're doing it in your home." So, she did. She walked through every room. Sat with us at the kitchen table. Asked all the big questions—our history, our values, our plans for parenting.

She gave us *nothing*. Total poker face. And the longer it went on, the more convinced we were that we'd blown it. We figured she'd go back to the agency, put a giant red X through our names, and tell them we couldn't even manage a dog, let alone a child.

Toward the end, she said, "I just want to check your basement one more time."

As I led her down the stairs, she turned halfway and looked back at me. "You know," she said, "a lot of people would've called to cancel today. They would've found some way to reschedule. But you just rolled with it." She smiled. "And really—what is parenting if not rolling with it?"

I swear, a hundred pounds of fear slid off my shoulders in that moment.

We passed.

Later that year, we were added to the "books"—the binder of approved families—and, eventually, three years later, in 2010, we got the call. A baby boy had been born in Virginia. His birth mom had chosen us.

Why? Because she saw our picture. The one with me, Patrick ... and Jackson.

And Jackson? He was the best big brother that boy could've had. Loyal, gentle, goofy. A constant companion until the day he passed, when our son was four.

To this day, I believe Jackson was part of the plan. The chaos, the couch, the skunk—all of it. Because he helped us tell the truth: We weren't perfect. We were *ready*.

Murder on Her Mind

Alice S. Marks

The doe's eyes seem to flash red as she fixes them on me. She raises her front legs in a manner that can't be mistaken as anything but menacing. Close-up, hooves that appeared so delicate at a distance show themselves to be sharp, lethal. An animal I'd always considered fragile and peaceful has turned livid, and I am the object of her wrath.

This event occurred in a woodland paradise at the end of our urban block. It commences with a waterfall cascading into Miller Creek, which empties into Lake Superior. A thick forest of evergreens and a variety of deciduous trees, as well as wildflowers and grasses, embellish either side of the stream. Outcroppings of boulders provide access to the water. A quaint wooden bridge provides a splendid view of the falls and allows hikers and bikers to cross over the stream to continue downward. Older folks like me choose a shorter, circular path.

The bike and walking paths on either side of the streams often allow views of wildlife, including squirrels, rabbits, chipmunks, and an occasional fox. Some visitors report having seen bears and a bobcat. I have glimpsed a couple of does deep in the woods. Until one terrifying day, I thought these female deer were Mother Nature's most beautiful, graceful, and peaceful animals.

My little dog and I are close to the end of our walk, which starts and ends at opposite sides of the falls. There was a grassy rise before we reached the end. A slight movement catches my attention. Under a tree, I see a small hollow, filled with leaves and moving white spots. A baby deer! I had no thought of moving closer to this glimpse of nature and was glad the dog, who is a bit dim-witted, didn't notice it.

As we resume walking, this gem of the moment ends as the baby's mother crashes into the scene. No grace nor placidness surrounds this animal. I drop the pup's leash so he can escape the out-of-control doe. Standing on her hind legs, she moves closer to me. She is poised to kick and stomp me with her raised front legs and sharp hooves. I move from her as I whisper, "I would never hurt your baby. I've had babies, and I understand why you see me as a threat."

I stumble on a rock, fall backward, make myself into a log, and begin rolling down a hill. I leave blood spatters from copious stickers and weeds as I move down a small hill, past the dog, who concentrates on a ladybug, oblivious to being free. At the bottom of the hill, I use a small tree to help me get up, which is the hardest thing for someone in her eighties to do after a fall. It takes several tries until I am upright. My dog still studies the bug as I reach him and snap the leash on. I limp home from the park as my little dog scampers along.

That fall and roll may have saved me by getting me out of the deer's view. I persist in telling my story to anyone I meet. A naturalist explained to me that if a female deer perceives her young are in danger, she will evolve from a gentle animal into a dangerous, stomping, kicking beast determined to kill. I find another listener to describe how I survived severe injuries or death when I encountered an incident of animal mayhem.

An Impawsible Mistake

Kelly McKenzie

It was your quintessential autumn day. Perfect for a stroll in the nearby forest. The towering cedar and pine trees provided shade from the sun, and the winding path was carpeted with crisp red, gold, and yellow maple leaves. It was as if someone had flung down several of the feathered cloaks favored by Hawaiian royalty. As I pulled my jacket tighter against the slight chill, Fergus, our eight-year-old black Lab, darted off the path to the small pond below. As always, the clean water called to him.

"Ferg, come back, boy. We don't have time!" I hollered.

That day's outing would have to be cut short. I'd promised to bring Bridget home for lunch. It was one of the monthly hot lunch days at school, and my second grader wasn't fond of today's pizza on offer. While I'd already prepared her chicken noodle soup and peanut butter sandwich, I needed to get back. She'd be upset if I arrived late.

A glistening rusty splotch on a pale, yellow leaf suddenly caught my eye. How beautiful. You really had to admire nature's color palette. As I pocketed the leaf to take home and preserve between the pages of a book, my fingers came away sticky. Was that blood? Ooph, yes. Had I somehow cut myself? No. Had Fergus? No, he returned to my side with his usual bounce, his tail wagging and tongue hanging out.

Even though a series of crimson spots continued to dot the path like the trail of breadcrumbs dropped by Hansel and Gretel, I dismissed all concerns regarding an injured innocent creature. We had to get home.

It was only when we wound our way up to the sidewalk that I was forced into a bit of a rethink. The now familiar pattern of claret-red paw prints were stamped onto the sidewalk. But only behind Fergus; there were *none* on the sidewalk ahead of him. My throat closed as I realized the truth. My poor dog was the injured party.

"Come here, boy," I crooned, my voice thick with guilt.

He trotted back, neither limping nor looking remotely distressed,

"I'm so sorry, Ferg. Let's have a look at you."

I lifted each paw gingerly, dreading each inspection, dearly hoping I was wrong. I wasn't.

He'd sliced through a pad on his back right paw. The cut was about the length of an office staple.

Shoot. The timing couldn't be worse. He clearly needed a stitch or ten, and Bridget would be waiting for me to pick her up. I couldn't be late. My poor darling would grow ever more anxious with each passing minute I didn't show. I needed a game plan.

Okay, I'd bandage the paw, alert the vet, get Bridget, return home, and bundle the patient off to medical attention. We could do this. Bridget could eat in the car and at the vet's. I had a good forty minutes before I had to get her back to school.

Not for the first time, I offered up thanks for my late husband's insistence that we possess a fully stocked first aid kit. If not for him, I would have treated Fergus with just two teeny Band-Aids, an ancient thermometer, and a dusty tongue depressor.

As Fergus first circled and then flopped onto his bed, I considered my options. Cotton squares, large ones. I ripped open several packets of white cotton bandage squares. I then dabbed at the ragged wound with one and placed three on his injury. Perfect. Holding them in place with one hand, I wrapped the beige stretchy bandage (intended for ankle sprains) tightly around the packed paw.

I appraised my efforts. While the floor still looked as if a ketchup bottle had exploded, the bandage was fresh. No blood was seeping through. Excellent. I swiped a damp cloth over the floor and tossed it into a nearby bucket.

"Okay, Ferg, you rest. I'm just going to zip up and get B. I won't be longer than ten minutes. Rest easy and we'll whip you off to the vet."

He thumped his tail in response.

Bridget broke into a huge smile as I strode to her classroom door. I willed myself to speak calmly. "Ferg has cut his paw on our walk, but I've bandaged it, love. We'll need to zip over to the vet's office. You can eat in the car."

Despite my best efforts, I sounded like a panicked captain ordering passengers to assemble at the muster station.

"How bad is it, Mom?" My seven-year-old, going on forty, asked with a worried frown.

"Not bad. He might need a stitch or two, but he'll be fine."

We returned to a murder scene. It was as if Charles Manson had escaped from prison. The floor was once again slick with blood. I couldn't believe it. Had Fergus yanked off the bandage? No. It was just as tightly bound as when I left. I was now thoroughly confused. How had I overlooked a more serious wound?

"I don't understand how I missed another cut, Bridge."

I grabbed the cloth from the bucket as she began to run her fingers over his body, like an experienced medic assessing for triage.

"Mom ..."

"I know you're hungry, Bridge, but we need to discover where he's hurt," I barked, my voice now sounding decidedly hoarse.

"Mom. Stop. Look at me."

I dragged my eyes from the floor just in time to catch a furtive exchange between my daughter and Fergus. He clearly viewed her as his champion; she'd make me understand. "What?"

"Mom, it's okay. Look. Fergus isn't hurt anywhere else."

"He isn't?"

"No. You've simply bandaged the wrong paw."

Who's the Mom?

Ryma Shohami

The day we brought our new dalmatian puppy, Maddie, home coincided with the day Missy, our lunatic cat (the vet's words, not mine!), decided it was the perfect time to proudly bring home her first litter of kittens, wherever she had been hiding them. One look at the canine intruder, and she flew into protective mommy mode. As far as Missy was concerned, she had carte blanche to claw out the dog's eyes. Fortunately, she failed in her mission.

The foiled attack was not an auspicious welcome for our distraught puppy, but she overcame and continued to stand up for her dignity. The emerging relationship between the two creatures was basically a cold war. There was much hissing and barking, but no blood was shed.

However, one of Missy's kittens, Mitzi, became smitten with Maddie, and the feelings were reciprocated; these two were inseparable.

Two years later, Mitzi became a mom to four gorgeous kittens. Unfortunately, Maddie was convinced the kittens were hers as well and tended to try to take over the mothering duties. Each tiny meow brought her running, whereupon she would proceed to wash the babies until they quieted down.

At five weeks, Mitzi decided that the little ones were ready for the outside world. She proudly led her brood down the stairs to our large back yard and proceeded to settle them in the shade of one of our huge trees. Just then, one of my daughters came outside with a chopped liver treat for Mitzi, who promptly abandoned the babies and headed for the goodies.

The kittens erupted into a chorus of distress, which brought Maddie zooming across the yard towards them. Unable to identify the precise danger to her charges, she adopted a belligerent stance and searched wildly in each direction for the attacker. At that point, Mitzi, also hearing the crying, headed back to the kittens. She found her way blocked by the dog, who not only wouldn't let her near the kittens, but for good measure, also chased her up the tree. And there she sat, crying pitifully for help.

Having watched this drama unfold from my kitchen window and seen my daughter helpless in the face of Maddie's hostile takeover of the brood, I snatched up the leash and marched outside.

"What is wrong with her!" wailed my daughter.

"I think she's suffering from Horton's Egg Syndrome," I laughed. Seeing the puzzled look on my daughter's face, I said, "You remember, Dr. Seuss, Maizie the lazy bird, Horton, elephant bird; oh, never mind."

It took a full minute to get the leash on Maddie and drag her away from the traumatized kittens.

After Mitzi maneuvered her way down from the tree and rounded up her babies, she walked haughtily past the leashed dog. Seeing that it was safe to do so, she hissed in Maddie's face as if to proclaim, "This friendship is over, you savage!"

Maddie hung her head in shame and spent the next several days trying to apologize to no avail. She would crawl cautiously toward the kittens whenever they cried, but one sharp look from Mitzi stopped her in her tracks.

Not until the kittens had grown a few more weeks and found their forever homes did Mitzi forgive her best friend.

Ratatouille

Renee Burns Lonner

I LIVE IN A SUBURBAN AREA OF LOS ANGELES ON A STREET lined with modest, neatly kept homes and yards. My housekeeping standards could be characterized as super-clean but definitely short of psychotic. You would guess that the word "rat" never enters my vocabulary when speaking about my house or yard.

You'd be wrong.

Several years ago, my gardener built a lovely vegetable planter in my backyard, and I planted all kinds of gourmet lettuces, herbs, and—my favorite—snow peas. They started to grow, and I was thrilled, like a farmer growing actual food to actually eat. I was so proud. Until I went out one morning and the lettuces had been eaten down to the nubs. The next morning, even the nubs were gone.

My neighborhood nursery is a second-generation family-owned business, and let me tell you, they know their stuff. I went in and described the problem, asked if there were raccoons suddenly in the area, and got a look like they thought I was somewhere between an imbecile and a moron.

One of the owners simply said, "Rats."

I replied, to his total amusement, "Can't be, rats don't eat lettuce!"

He sighed a patient sigh and said, "They eat anything and everything." Who knew?

Not to be outsmarted by a rodent, at the end of that season, I asked the gardener to build a four-foot-high raised vegetable bed and put a little fence around it. (You're thinking, "She's closer to imbecile than moron.")

That following winter, I planted another round of beautiful lettuces. Same outcome, only that time, it took less than a week. I was angry. I went to the hardware store and bought chicken wire and crafted a cage for the lettuces—which are by now the most expensive greens in California. Made a small door I could open (with difficulty and some bleeding) to harvest my crop.

What crop? Within a day or two of my construction project and *before* my cuts healed, same result.

OKAY ... THAT MEANT WAR!

My husband, who had been muttering something that may have sounded like "rat traps" for over a year, again offered his services. By then, I no longer objected "because it was inhumane." Instant death by guillotine sounded perfect.

My husband set up several traps and, the next morning, calmly announced that he had caught two and had already disposed of them, and that my new lettuces were undisturbed. My hero!

Over the next week, he caught a couple more, and then it was all quiet. His theory was that when the "scouts" did not return, the group got the message to avoid that murderer's yard! Clearly, they were reading my Nextdoor feed.

Fast forward, and a horrifying discovery when I opened the closet in my guest house. Yup, you guessed it—a rat dropping. After I finished screaming to an empty room in an empty guest house, my husband set a trap where the dropping was. Simultaneously, I called pest control. This was no longer a job for amateurs. I needed SWAT-style backup.

The company responded to my near hysteria with, "We have a *special* rat guy, Reuben. *He'll* solve your problem." Yes, I needed special forces, THAT was the answer.

When Reuben arrived the next morning, he asked the most bizarre question as he looked at our trap: "Is that peanut butter in the trap *organic*?" Wait, WHHAAAT?? I looked at him like one of us had lost their minds, and *this* time it wasn't me. He added, "They won't eat that organic crap." Good news for Reuben, neither will I.

The next thing I knew, Reuben was on the roof of my guest house. Soon, he knocked on my door, and when I answered, he had the look of someone who had just slayed a dragon. Which he had. "I found where he (gender noted) is getting in! Come with me!"

I followed him and he excitedly showed me a *tiny* hole near the foundation of the guest house, then trotted, with his finger pointing, along "the route," and finally triumphantly showed me the inside landing place. He pointed to rat droppings that were too high for me to see as proof of his detective work.

I was impressed. He, in a totally smug voice, told me the—not minor—cost of his services to rodent-proof the guest house over the next couple of hours. Worth every penny.

As he left, he told me that rats were everywhere in the city. Apparently, the Big Apple has nothing on Los Angeles. Every yard has them, and yes, they often get into houses. That revelation took care of my embarrassment about the whole situation. Never mind rodent-proof, he had an everything-proof business. Apparently, we all live in rat-infested cities. How reassuring.

One of our friends, to whom I told this entire story in long form, lives fifty miles from us, out in the country, on a large property with its own zoo: horses, cats, dogs, tortoises, a bird or two. His smart-ass response when I told him the rat saga was, "For heaven's sake, Renee —get a cat. I'll give you one of mine."

A "Scent-sational" Skunk Secret

Glenda Ferguson

EACH SPRING, I ENJOYED WATCHING THE SKUNK (JUST ONE) ON our property, but only from a distance. Something about that little mammal's black nose sniffing the ground for sunflower seeds around our bird feeding stations fascinated me. As for my husband Tim, he wanted the little odor eater barred from our yard and limited to the woods bordering our one acre. In all the forty years living here in southern Indiana, we only witnessed one skunk at a time. Fortunately, each year, the skunk moved on to a new location before Tim took action.

However, two months ago, I witnessed skunks (more than one).

In April, Tim hurt his back. He wasn't able to mow the lawn or even sit on the screened back porch with our kitten, Scrappy. He still wanted to hear all about the wildlife that visited daily. So, I described the gentle doe and her spotted twin fawns. I listed the variety of songbirds at the feeders. I told him about the rare flock of wild turkeys, with three adults and ten juveniles, foraging the grass on their way to the field next to us.

But I didn't tell him about the mama skunk and her four black-and-white kits appearing each morning.

Scrappy alerted me to their early visits when our ever-hungry cat didn't pop in for her breakfast as usual. When I opened the back door, Scrappy was crouched down and fixated on some dark shadows next to the garage. I stepped closer and called her name. She scurried further down the porch. That's when I also saw the shadows moving. Five of them waddled as a group under the bird feeders. The only occasion I had witnessed a skunk mother with her little ones was from a distance. Never up close. I knew the situation could get personal if Scrappy or I startled the mama. We froze. This was a rare opportunity to view their behavior as all four stayed close to their mother.

I knew what my tabby and I had to do. We must not mention the black-and-white visitors. Tim would be disgusted by just the mention of them. Then that stinker husband of mine would devise a plan for making sure the skunk family left our property and never returned.

That didn't stop Scrappy and me from being thrilled by the sight of the family. Each morning, from our screened back porch, we would quietly find a secluded vantage point and watch their antics. We were captivated by the striped quintet nosing around the sunflower seeds scattered on the ground. The group of adorable youngsters considered searching for food and playtime, but serious mama was all about feeding her little black-and-white beauties. Regarding the group's unpleasant smell, everyone refrained from spraying.

While Tim recovered, and the little kits matured, Scrappy and I kept our guilty pleasure a secret. I researched how the family would move along in early June and find more suitable locations.

One morning, they were gone. I was sad to see them go. Scrappy missed our skunk viewings, too. But the timing was perfect. Tim had healed and wished to get back into his routine of doing yard work. Scrappy and I had dodged any telltale signs that we had multiple skunks on our one acre.

Or so we thought.

One week later, I woke up to the distinct odor of skunk. Tim caught a whiff of it, too. I was nervous that the family was back, and he would discover them. But Tim left for work without thinking anything was unusual. The smell dissipated, and I supposed the animal(s) left.

The next morning, the odor was back.

This time, after Tim left, I investigated outside near the bedroom window. That's where the scent grew more dreadful. Right under the window was our cellar, covered with a heavy metal door. As I approached, the odor rose from underground. I noticed a hole dug under the frame. Something, apparently the skunk, clawed an opening leading down the wooden staircase. Our cellar door at the bottom of the stairs must have slammed shut. The skunk was trapped and sent out a smelly SOS. I sniffed the seriousness of the situation. There was no way I could open the steel door alone. I needed reinforcements.

When Tim returned home, I pleaded with him for help. I didn't alert him that he may discover not one, but several skunks. It was risky, but I could pretend to be surprised also by the multitude of skunks.

Tim tiptoed down the unsteady steps and slowly opened the door. Sure enough, he found what was causing the unpleasant smell. Just one skunk. The stuck skunk smelled freedom and dashed up the steps to safety into the woods. I was relieved there was a solitary skunk, but also proud of how exceptionally beautiful one of the little kits had turned out.

As far as I know, Scrappy never revealed our skunk secret to Tim, and neither have I.

The King Has Left the Driveway

Amy Mullis

I'm pretty sure I have a target shaped like a filet mignon stuck on my back with edible glue. Or there is a flashing neon sign that says EASY MARK over my house in letters that only animals can see. Or maybe there's a bulletin board somewhere in the neighborhood where wandering creatures check for lodging when they're looking for a place to bunk for the night, and a wayward tabby cat has given me five stars. Somewhere a Labrador is saying, "*Hmmm,* two bedrooms, one bath, dinner at eight. I have just enough time to soil their lawn before I scratch at their door." However, the system works; I have always been a rest stop on the stray animal highway.

Once they stop to sniff the bacon, they usually decide to stay. I serve regular meals, and there are always treats in the drawer. As a result, my house has been home to an ever-changing blended family, and I've found that any mix of animals can learn to coexist peacefully —well, almost peacefully—as long as they understand the house rules.

Regulars at my bird feeders invite their distant relatives like a sort of feathered family reunion. At the same time, feral cats recline in my porch rockers, yawning and checking their stomach clocks, until room service arrives to fill their bowls for breakfast. Two labradors and a dachshund later, I'm on my last rescue animal (if last means the one sprawled on his own sofa with two pillows to cushion his head), a pit bull mix so gentle my two-year-old niece gives him bear hugs and instructs him when to play with his nylon bone. He was trained in community manners by a tiny kitten who had more attitude than latitude.

Then there was the snake.

When I wheeled into my driveway one afternoon, I wasn't surprised to find a new face waiting at the end of the driveway. I was surprised that it belonged to a snake.

I get along with snakes like I get along with sea creatures on family trips to the beach. They are graceful and awe-inspiring in their own environments, but when they swim close enough to nibble my toes, I'm ready to chuck the whole adventure and go for ice cream. I've never had a nibble on my piggies, but I have had lots of double chocolate cones to pass the time.

I slipped out of my car to take the short walk across the road to the mailbox when I saw him.

And he saw me.

My mailbox waited across the road, possibly full of exciting offers and prize notifications. But I had to walk past the snake to get to it.

And he was big. Big in the way that drawings of superheroes have muscles that make the rest of us look like drinking straws. He was black, with a thin white diamond pattern that ran tip to tail, and his body was doubled up here and there, in a way that reminded me of my dad's folding ruler that opened to five times its storage size. Not a thought to inspire courageous action. Later, I would identify him as a king snake, the best kind of guy to have around to take care of the sort of pesky snakes who sunbathe in the garden waiting for a chance to snack on your ankle. At a distance, he was beautiful.

But he wasn't distant enough.

I subscribe to the Live and Let Live theory, but since I had never had the opportunity to pick his sort out of a snake lineup, I felt like the "distance makes the heart grow fonder" theory applied.

I wasn't sure he felt the same way.

I took a timid step toward the mailbox with the idea that tiptoeing is nonthreatening, when he moved. He was probably just stretching to get a kink out of his neck or scratch an itch, but I took it personally.

There's a special dance that comes with finding an unexpected creature in your personal space. It involves uninhibited movement of the hands and feet and is sometimes accompanied by the loss of bodily fluids. I immediately launched into that dance.

In cartoons, when characters get frightened, they disappear in a cloud, accompanied by a funny noise indicating a rapid departure. My noise was not of the cartoon variety, but my departure beat known speed records. I'm hoping my Tarzan-like scream covered up any telltale bodily explosions as I slammed into the car door over and over until, by luck, I landed back in the driver's seat. One foot was stuck in my pocketbook, and it took three tries to close the window so the snake couldn't get in, but fortunately, that snake was not equipped for flight.

As I squealed down the driveway and slid to a stop, I checked my rearview mirror to see if the enemy was advancing.

The snake shrugged his shoulders and eased toward the drain that led to the undeveloped plot of land down the hill.

And I swear he was laughing.

My Starter Pet
Jennifer Priest Mitchell

When I was in my twenties, I lived near my brother and his wife, and their small tribe of sweet pets, which included a cat. Once, after a difficult week, I spent a few days with them. I alternated between crying, drinking amazing black tea with cream, and cuddling their little black cat, Bullet, who truly comforted me. Soft nuzzles, her sashay up to graze my calves, and her gentle purr in my ear opened my heart to the world of felines.

I lived alone and had never had a pet. Shortly after falling in love with Bullet the cat, I decided to become a cat person. I was soon on the lookout for a kitten to adopt and eventually found a family whose cat had a litter. I selected a playful gray female and named her Pip after the character from Charles Dickens's *Great Expectations*. From humble beginnings to a charmed life with me, Pip was going to be my new best friend.

Pip and I grew quite close as she was my first roommate after college. She had habits I didn't adore, but I loved how she greeted me cheerfully each day when I returned from work and kept me company all evening. Her behavior, however, included shredding paper, which was a challenge for me as I owned many books, notebooks, magazines, and newspapers. My countertops housed baskets of bills and assorted mail, all tempting Pip. Still, I loved her and was committed to making our relationship work.

I tried to place paper items far from her reach. I provided her with toys to occupy her nights when she mangled, in a festive, playful manner, any paper that had inadvertently been left available. Pip's talents expanded, and she eventually learned to withdraw books from tightly packed shelves. She ended up modifying cookbooks, library books, and an old Bible. She didn't destroy books, but she did update their appearances. I continued to try to meet Pip where she was by purchasing a scratching pole, a climbing pole, and even some compact discs of music whose labels claimed the tunes would calm anxious pets.

Over time, in the absence of paper and among the dozen or so distractions I had purchased and set up for her, Pip developed a new habit. She would perch on top of my refrigerator near the back door. Any time someone new entered the apartment, she sprang into action and pounced, landing on the guest's shoulder. Pip had claws. She had moxie. Eventually, what she didn't have was fans.

After landing on someone's shoulder, she'd gently rub their neck with her tiny pink nose, attempting to befriend them, but the initial meeting often spurred the recipient of this misguided affection to swat at Pip. This led to a new response from Pip: biting. Always provoked, never aimed at me, but still, biting. These were not blood-drawing bites, but they did help me realize which friends had the most patience.

I continued to seek the right balance of toys, affection, and distractions to ease Pip's nervousness and diffuse her energy, which I have always interpreted as love. One time when my parents from out of town visited us, Pip darted out the apartment door as we unloaded the car. My dad and I spent hours walking the German Village neighborhood of Columbus, Ohio, in search of her. This was a difficult task as the area was full of mature trees and lush flowers. It was midsummer when everything was bushy and full, providing ample cover for my seemingly wild kitty.

My dad opened the back door and kept running the electric can opener I used to open canned food for Pip on occasion. He thought that the sound, which always brought my cat to the kitchen, might lure her in from outside. Dusk fell, and we began to work on signs to post on telephone poles, announcing her as missing and asking people to phone me if they saw her.

"Wait a minute!" my dad called from the kitchen where he'd been steadily hitting the can opener in hopes of her return. "I think I hear her!"

We both stepped out to the patio beyond my building, and heard her soft, peepy, "Mew."

"Pip!" I cried. There she was, curled into a soft gray ball right near my back door. For the first time in her three years of life, she remained still as I scooped her up and brought her in for a hug. She was a little muddy, so we gently wiped her down. I wondered how far she had gone and what she had experienced.

Later that evening, my parents got ready for bed and retreated to my bedroom as I stretched out on the daybed in my living room. Pip began her nighttime routine in which she would slink about, looking for paper or other things I didn't want her to have, solidly ignoring all her cat toys. She finally settled in and slept near my feet on top of the covers, where she continued to sleep most nights. I think her outdoor adventure calmed her a bit.

In the coming year, I got engaged and then married, and amid all the excitement of those changes, I found a new home for Pip—someplace where she had lots of company, both human and feline. The family who adopted her provided her with designated paper to work with. Why hadn't I thought of that?

The tender, ongoing task of working with Pip and meeting her where she was turned out to be great preparation for my later relationships with a series of dogs, another cat I fostered, some fish, frogs, and, eventually our children. Pip was a gateway pet, a starter pet for me, showing me how to be less consumed with myself. She was the first being in my life who truly inspired me to try and meet someone else exactly where they are.

I still reflect on my young adult years, trying to stay one step ahead of Pip the cat and providing distractions and joys for her, anticipating which situations and physical comforts would bring out the best in her. This skill is something I continue to hone as a wife, mother, daughter, sister, employee, and friend, but the foundation of this journey all began with a soft gray kitten, so whimsical and playful, named Pip.

A Fish Out of Water

Liz Sheahan

One Saturday when our oldest son, Nick, was in second grade, we attended the school carnival. The gym was packed with activities for the whole family—a cake walk, silent auction, food, relays, and the Ping-Pong ball toss, in which kids had a chance to throw a ball into a target of small fish bowls. If they were lucky enough to get their ball into one of the bowls, they got a prize. Nick was quite skilled at this game and won two certificates from the pet store—each for a FREE goldfish! He was thrilled.

At the end of the day, with our bellies full and a bag full of winnings, we headed home. When I finally had a chance to go through the bag, I stuck the two certificates on the fridge with a magnet.

After several months of waiting, sweet Nickolas inquired, "Can we please go get my goldfish?"

And so, Nick, his little brother Joey, and I ventured the mile to the pet store. I envisioned two little fish in a small, round bowl and a few colorful stones in the bottom.

As we were peering into the big aquariums full of a wide variety of aquatic creatures that lined one wall, a clerk approached us with a smile. Bright-eyed in anticipation, Nick showed her his two hard-earned certificates. She helped him pick out two fish—one was a beefier goldfish, and the other had more frilly fins. He decided to name the former one Max (short for Maximum) and the fluffier, more petite one Mini (short for Minimum).

I walked toward the round fish bowls, but the clerk cheerfully redirected me—she let me know we needed a larger aquarium for the fish. With great confidence and authority, she shared the equation for the number of gallons per inch of fish that were required for the little beings to have a healthy habitat and then pointed us toward the more substantial tanks.

Nick and Joey were thrilled—this was going to be so cool!

A few little stones in the bottom weren't going to accomplish what was needed for this tank, so we picked out a bag of aqua-colored stones, and, of course, a wrecked pirate ship the fish could hide in, and some plastic seaweed to fill the vast space, as well as the required food for these little critters.

Adding up the cost of these free goldfish in my head, I let the clerk know we didn't need a cover or a pump, as I would make sure the water stayed clean. After all, what young working mother doesn't have time to clean out a fish tank a couple of times every week? What else could I possibly have to do after the kids go to bed?

We took Max and Mini home to join our family. Their rectangular glass abode sat on top of the dresser in Nick's room, where they could watch him play, and he could see them from his bed.

While I hated cleaning out the tank, I did come to really love those fish—they would swim around excitedly whenever I walked into the room. They recognized that I was the being who fed them and cared for them. Who doesn't love being loved?

Both fish grew quite a bit, but we could tell they were aptly named. Max got to be twice the size of Mini, and while she'd grown, she maintained her flowy, feminine look. (*Side note: We did have another family member—Princess, our beloved collie. And, I was working full-time, so the house wasn't always as clean and organized as those portrayed in the magazines in the checkout lane at the grocery store.)*

Early one Saturday morning, I was shaken awake by Nick and Joey, who were standing at my bedside. "Mom!" they exclaimed frantically, "We can't find Mini!"

I was foggy, still longing for sleep, but needed to assure my kids that their pet fish was fine. I didn't have my contacts in yet but followed them through the house to Nick's room.

The day before, Nick and I had gotten a start on organizing his toys, so there were half a dozen brown paper grocery bags in which we were sorting toys all pushed around the base of his dresser (upon which the aquarium was perched).

With Nick and Joey anxiously watching me, I squinted through the glass ... big Max was swimming around happily, but I did not see his sister. I stuck my hand into the tepid water and gently shook the pirate ship, thinking she surely was hiding inside. Nothing. I carefully dug my fingers into the aqua-colored stones and swished them around a bit. No sign of the frilly little fish.

Then I looked carefully into each of the grocery bags that sat on the floor, but still no evidence of Mini.

Having come in there directly from my cozy bed, I really needed to use the bathroom. I excused myself, and when I came around the corner back into the bedroom, my eyes were drawn to a small, pale, tan-colored mass on the carpet next to the base of the dresser.

As I reached down, I said, "Oh-oh," fearing the worst. The boys were right beside me, looking fearful and sad.

With my somewhat blurry vision, I touched the little mass and let out a high-pitched scream as it jumped!

I quickly picked it up—Mini was wrapped like a mummy in Princess's long hair! As I dropped Mini into the fish tank, she spun around as the dog hair unraveled from her little body—we were all shocked and amazed at the sight of her swimming around with Max. She was missing a couple of tiny scales but otherwise was unscathed.

So little Mini had jumped out of the aquarium, landed on the carpet, and tossed around enough to wrap her up in the dog's hair, which preserved her until she was found. It was truly miraculous!

After that, I never felt too guilty for not vacuuming often enough. I did, however, purchase a lid for the aquarium.

The Great Lasagna Heist

Mona Smith

I REMEMBER THIS CULINARY THIEVERY WELL. THE PERPS WERE cool, cunning, and cuddly: Nicolas, my Newfie-mix pup, and his web-footed cohort in crime, Newton, a house duck who wore a diaper.

My work was short-staffed, and I was pulling long shifts, meaning I missed my husband's famous lasagna dinner. He managed to save me a slice. Having a pup and a duck in the house is like having two toddlers on espresso. I wanted to savor my slice, so I put the two future thieves on the couch and turned on their favorite show, *Barney*.

Who knew a giant purple dinosaur could entertain the two as they snuggled on the couch? I was waiting to hear the ding of the microwave to announce my delectable piece of heaven was warmed and ready to eat.

Nicolas and Newton were great pals—or should I say conspirators. I watched as Nicolas leaned closer toward Newton, who quacked softly in his ear. I thought it was sweet. It wasn't sweet—they were hatching a plan for the amazing heist.

The microwave dinged, and the delicious aroma wafted out as I removed my lunch. I decided to sit in the oversized armchair and watch *Barney* with my odd-couple pets.

As I was about to take the first bite, a curious thing happened: Nicolas barked. Nicolas never barks.

"What's wrong?" I asked him. He whined. I placed my cooling plate of lasagna on the coffee table and went to check on Nicolas. I sat next to him, scratching behind his ears—his favorite spot. He closed his eyes as I continued to rub.

"That's all you needed." Then the thought came to me like a train without brakes going downhill in an ice storm. Where was Newton? He wasn't on the couch. He wasn't in front of the TV. I keep telling Newton he's going to go blind sitting that close to the TV. His response is to quack gibberish at me. He thinks I don't know he's telling me off, but I know. I needed to find my web-footed troublemaker.

I quit rubbing behind Nicolas's ears, and he opened his eyes. "Nicolas, where is Newton?"

Nicolas was always a well-behaved pup. His eyes told me he didn't want to rat out his friend. "Nicolas, tell me where Newton is."

He looked toward the coffee table. That's when a little white head and orange bill popped up. Newton was close to my plate of lasagna.

"Don't even think of it," I said in my "do it and you will be covered in orange sauce" voice. Newton knows it's an empty threat, and I haven't a clue why I think it will work this time.

Newton cocked his head and winked at me. Yes, my duck winks. He jumped onto the coffee table, let out the loudest quack, and dove for my lasagna. Nicolas jumped off the couch as Newton grabbed my lasagna and made his escape. His bill was full of my slice, making his quack a muffled call for Nicolas to follow. I almost caught him when Nicolas cut me off. Down the hall the hooligans took flight—Newton with his wings spread like an eagle soaring, Nicolas not far behind. They headed for the living room. I was in hot pursuit.

There was pasta sauce on the floor and the walls as I made my way down the hall. When I reached the living room, the lasagna thieves had consumed most of the spoils of their heist.

I glanced around the room. Globs of sauce and cheese were the only things left of my slice.

I spied a lone lasagna noodle and picked it up. I wasn't planning to eat it—but that wasn't an option anyway. As quickly as I picked it up, an orange bill snatched it from my hand. I watched Newton swallow the noodle like a worm in the yard. He then winked at me.

Ruff Nights

January Gordon Ornellas

My 107-year-old dog, Dixie (who barely looks a day over 98), had become sweet and mellow in her old age. This wasn't always the case. Once upon a time, Dixie was deemed a "Nuisance Dog" because she may have gotten into a kerfuffle or two. This led to a court appearance, after which animal control mandated that Dixie wear a nuisance collar ... FOREVER! (Sidenote: How about collars for "Nuisance Adults?")

The whole thing was pretty unfair because Dixie was sixteen at the time, and who among us hasn't made some poor choices in our teenage years? The good news is that Dixie eventually grew out of her antics and matured into an upstanding canine who causes us little grief.

Until two weeks ago.

It started with Dixie waking ME (Steve was conveniently out of town) in the middle of the night. At first, it was just once a night to go to the bathroom.

I get it, Dixie. Our bladders aren't what they used to be.

But this quickly evolved into several times a night. Some nights,

Dixie didn't even go to the bathroom. Instead, she would just sit on the front lawn, staring into space, deep in thought.

Dixie, you don't have any deep thoughts. YOU'RE A DOG!

Other nights, Dixie would head down the driveway, insistent on a 2:00 a.m. walk.

"Get back in the house!" I yelled.

But Dixie weaved and dodged as I chased her up the driveway. I guess I was "It."

Under bushes, I scrambled. Across the lawn, I sprinted. It didn't help that it was raining. At one point, she slipped from my grasp, and I face-planted on the grass. (Highlights of this footage can be seen on our Ring video.)

An hour later, I managed to coax her inside. She immediately ran to the treat bowl.

"If you think you're getting a treat for what you just did, you are sadly mistaken, Missy!" I folded my arms, so she knew *who was boss!*

Then I gave her a treat, and we called it a night.

The following evening, Steve returned from his business trip.

"If you want something in the middle of the night," I whispered into Dixie's ear, "Daddy's your guy."

At a quarter to one, Dixie scratched on my side of the bed. I groaned. "We just went over this, Dixie." Then I picked her up, placed her on Steve's side, and returned to bed.

Scratch, scratch, scratch.

I elbowed Steve. "Dixie wants you."

This continued for several nights, with Dixie waking us every two hours.

"It's your turn!"

"No, it's your turn!"

"No, I was just up; it's your turn!"

It was like having a newborn. However, at least with a newborn, that angelic face you gaze into at 2:00 a.m. cushions the blow. (Dixie just read this and she's pissed!)

Dixie, you, too, have the face of an angel. If I implied otherwise, I apologize.

The second week, Dixie found new ways to amuse us at 3:00 a.m.

Instead of roaming the front lawn, she took to roaming the hallways. With her long nails and our wood floors, it was a steady stream of clickety-clacks, like we had a tiny Clydesdale prancing through our house.

All night long, Dixie clickety-clacked from room to room, in search of a bed that was *just right.*

Unfortunately, one was too hard, and one was too soft, so around 4:00 a.m., Dixie went downstairs. *Click-Click-Clickety-Clack.*

Both of us were wide awake and staring at the ceiling as Dixie tap danced across the kitchen tile.

"What is she doing?" Steve asked.

I sighed. "Looking for porridge?"

Dixie soon returned to our room, but instead of jumping into our bed, she burrowed beneath it. There was some initial scratching on the box spring, followed by pounding, and then what can only be described as drilling. It sounded as if Dixie was building shelves under our bed.

Can Dixie operate power tools? I put nothing past that dog.

The next day, in a sleep-deprived stupor, I took Dixie to the vet.

"She's doing great for her age," the vet said. "But she could be experiencing some sundowning."

The vet suggested we try Benadryl, melatonin, or hemp.

Unfortunately, the first two didn't work, and Dixie refused to even try the hemp.

"Trust me, baby, you're going to love it," I said, holding out my hand. "All the other dogs are doing it."

Dixie walked away. Apparently, she says *nope to the dope.*

After another sleepless week, the vet prescribed something called trazodone, which was supposed to reduce anxiety and provide a good night's sleep.

Can I have some?

At first, Dixie wasn't interested, but when I asked, "Do you want to make it to your one hundred fourteenth birthday?" she changed her tune.

Now, every night around eight o'clock, I slip a pill in a piece of sweet Italian sausage, and Dixie sleeps like a pup.

No more nocturnal Dixie!

But then last week, I tried to slip her pill in a hot dog, she gave me that look.

I ordered sausage trazodone, not hotdog trazodone.

So, I immediately cooked her up some sausage because, let's be honest, we all know Dixie's running the show.

In fact, some might even call her the boss.

Just don't call her a nuisance.

The Closet Chronicles of Alexandria

(Thunder, Teeth, and Trousers)

Ryan Hale

ALEXANDRIA—ALEX FOR SHORT—WAS NOT MERELY A PET. SHE was a presence. A red Doberman with beige-colored brows that lifted in curiosity or concern, depending on the tone of my voice. At eighty-five pounds, she had no idea she was a dog. I suspect she thought she was a very small, warm human with a stubby tail and a wet nose, genetically obligated to sit in my lap the moment I sat down.

She didn't just sit in my lap—she melted into it. Like a pot of red molasses, she slathered her full weight across me with one long exhale, waiting for her ears to be rubbed for love and comfort. That was our nightly routine. I'm in the recliner. Alex was on my lap. If there was ever a moment of true contentment in this world, it was found in that chair, during those hours, with her head tucked beneath my chin and the television flickering in front of us.

Alex was a study in contradictions. She was protective in posture and timid in practice. She was a canine paradox of the most remarkable example. If someone rang the doorbell, she'd beat me to the door —head high, shoulders squared, low growl rumbling in her chest. But the moment the door cracked open and someone stepped in, she'd retreat behind me like a toddler meeting Santa Claus for the first time. Fierce from afar, cautious up close.

I often joked that we could be robbed by anyone with mean eyes and a vacuum cleaner, because both sent Alex into hiding. My older brother was visiting one afternoon, arriving while Alex was outside taking care of her business. When Alex came in, it was the first time she and my brother, nicknamed "Uncle Scary Eyes" that day, had ever met. She stopped in her tracks and started barking ferociously and protectively of me. I, of course, was sitting safely in my reclining position.

Alex stopped barking as soon as my brother gave her a mean-eyed look. She began to back away from him, inching slowly toward the bottom of my feet. My brother thought it was funny, so he stood slowly from the sofa. Alex pushed her rear end onto my feet. Using only her front paws, she continued to move, sliding her tail back and up until her butt came to rest on my right shoulder. Her front paws were buried into my stomach, and she looked from my brother to me as if asking me if I would stop the evil man from approaching.

My brother and I had a good laugh, and then he rubbed her face and ears to show Alex that he was lovable, too, blessed with expressive eyes. So expressive that day, they gave me an eighty-five-pound, shoulder-sitting Doberman parrot.

Alex was brilliant, too! We all believe our fur babies are smart, attributing human thoughts to their expressions and reactions to things happening around them. Alex could do the standard sit, shake, lie down (never caught on to roll over), and howl along to a tune with my daughter. One of her best tricks was closing doors. She would come into our room at night to go to bed–the bed she allowed my wife and me to sleep in—and we would say, "Close the door." Alex would stop and use only her head to gently close the door! It was remarkable! But we would find out later that every door was not so gently closed.

Texas is known for having big everything. Big ranches, oil reserves, cities, hair, and massive storms. Tornadoes, hurricanes, flashfloods, damaging straight-line winds, dust-devils, lightning, and hail the size of softballs. You name it, and we get it. And Alex was not a fan of it. It didn't require much to upset her. God help us when the clouds rolled in.

Rain didn't need to fall heavily, for even a light mist would do it. Lightning didn't need to flash. Just the low atmospheric shift that made the hair on your arms rise was felt in her marrow. The first roll of distant thunder would send her into a panic that made my wife and me drop whatever we were doing and run to see that our closet door was closed, and Alex remained close to us. That was never an issue when we were home because she would seek us out for protection from the elemental onslaught Alex anticipated.

The problem arose when my wife and I were working when the clouds rolled in. You see, Alex had devised her version of a storm shelter. It wasn't the bathtub. It wasn't under the bed. No, it was the protective confines of our master closet. She'd dart inside with the grace of a greyhound and use her strong front paws—those pincher paws worthy of her breed's name—to shut the door behind her. Not halfway. Not gently nudged with her soft, pointed muzzle. Full. Slam. Shut. It took us a few storms to realize she had taught herself how to close doors but not how to open them again.

And that's when the real damage began.

Alex, bless her panic-stricken heart, didn't do well in isolation. Anxiety quadrupled when she was locked in. She'd start with the pants. Always the pants. My wife's pants. Hanging in perfect military alignment, creased and starched on the lower rod. Alex would go one by one, using those front teeth to nip through the center of the crease with surgical precision. Pants were ruined in clusters—usually eight to ten pairs per rainstorm—a simple slice through the front of both legs and *voila,* destroyed jeans.

Then came the stomach upset. Apparently, dread curdles a Doberman's guts like spoiled milk. Whatever she had eaten earlier came back up—or out—often into the open mouths of my favorite leather shoes. If they were polished leather, they doubled as reflective bowls. Once done, she'd run frantic circles in the confined space, ensuring her offerings touched as many surfaces as possible—closet carpet, hems of shirts, the back of the door—everywhere! When we pried the door open, the smell alone was enough to kill a houseplant. The scene? A Salvador Dali painting interpreted by a hysterical dog with diarrhea.

It was in those moments, just like with all our children, that parentage was declared. My wife would look at me and say, "See what *your* dog did—again!" There were many major cleanups in the clothing aisle with carpet cleaners, rubber gloves, and nose plugs. And yet ... I never stayed mad at Alex. I couldn't. Not when I looked into those apologetic, brown eyes. Not when she tucked her head into my chest and whined as if to say, "I didn't mean to. I couldn't help it." Or more accurately, "I forgive you for letting it rain on my house. You have been punished enough, so rub my ears—you'll feel better."

She couldn't help it. And I couldn't help loving her.

Years later, I still pause during storms, looking at the closet door, half expecting to see a brown nose pushing it shut behind her. We learned from Alex's trauma. Now that we are retired, rain or shine, we are always with our doodle, and our closet door is always closed.

An Open Letter to the Zebra That Bit My Seven-Year-Old at the County Fair

Caroline Horwitz

First of all, I want to assert that I in no way blame you, a poor, confused ungulate nearly eight thousand miles away from the Serengeti. What, I'm sure you were wondering, were you doing sharing a barnyard pen with two camels and a baby wildebeest in rural Pennsylvania?

You seemed so receptive at first to our cautious approach and gentle pets, so eager to make friends as you adorably stretched your head toward us. Were you just luring us in with a false sense of security? You probably thought we had food for you—at least, that's how I rationalized it to my kid, so let's stick with that, yeah? No need to make it personal. In our defense, we *would've* had food for you had the pygmy goats not greedily gobbled all of our petting-zoo pellets beforehand.

I mean, hey, I get it. You're an undomesticated animal—you bite for reasons humans can't always understand. I'm not about to question the self-preservation instincts of a creature who's biologically programmed to anticipate lion and crocodile attacks.

It's just that ... you're actually my seven-year-old's favorite animal. Well, *were*. Let's be honest here. And how often is one afforded the opportunity to pet a real-life zebra? It was a magical childhood moment in the making! I guess you could say this was an early lesson of the "Don't Meet Your Heroes" variety.

Also, did you have to nip him the half second before I snapped the picture of you together? Now, instead of a sweet visual memento of my youngest child petting his favorite critter, I have photographic evidence of him exclaiming in shock and pain as you turn your muzzle away. (Out of context, I suppose, someone could mistake his expression for being ***really*** excited.)

No offense, but you totally missed your golden opportunity to make it onto our holiday card or next year's family photo calendar. I'm sure you're crushed.

I guess my son might find this picture funny in ten years. Either that or he'll use it to put me on blast on whatever social media app the future Gen Alpha teens are using then.

Seriously, though, no hard feelings. You didn't even break the skin. Had I allowed my oldest son to bring those carnival-game goldfish home, you wouldn't even have been the most traumatic animal event of the weekend.

My seven-year-old assures me that he harbors no ill feelings toward you, although he did casually remark during the car ride home that your bite was his least favorite part of the fair and that red pandas are now his new favorite animals.

I should probably remind myself never to partake should the zoo decide to host some sort of meet-and-greet with those.

All the best in your striped life,

Caroline

Misunderstood Piggy

Robin Raniero Norris

When I was growing up, I lived on an island and didn't really have any pets for my first fifteen years. The nature outside became my friends—or food. I watched the majestic swans come in for graceful water landings. I listened to the geese's never-ending honking. I made *squaw* sounds along with the seagulls as they laughed in the skies. Some of my days were spent fishing, crabbing, and moving my feet around in the muddy muck of the water to capture a dinner of steamers. We called them "spit clams" because they were constantly spewing water from their siphons. I never thought I would live somewhere not close to or on the water. But I got married and live in a community that is all about the land. All turf, no surf.

One day, my children came home and said they wanted to join a local agricultural group. I was intrigued for sure. Who doesn't want to understand more about how honey is made? I thought we would grow some plants on the windowsill. Perhaps we could even create some useful things for our community.

The joke was on me. Soon after my little ol' Pollyanna voice said, "Yes," a four-legged critter that I felt could eat me alive or at least trample me to death after it knocked me down, showed up at our house. Somehow, I had agreed to the "pig" assignment.

The extent of my knowledge about swine, *sus scrofa domesticus,* more commonly known to us lay people as pigs, came from *Charlotte's Web* or the Pixar movies featuring a boy and his flying space toy, where one of the supporting characters was a witty, sarcastic piggy bank named Ham. I felt like a confident driver ready to conquer the world on day two with a learner's permit.

A black-and-white piglet arrived at our house in January. I was told that it would depart in early spring, which gave me mixed emotions. Since it was the middle of winter, into our shop he went, secured in a makeshift wooden structure we filled with straw, water, and food. Oh, and heat lamps. (I'm pretty sure our electric company sent us a thank-you card after the winter season.) The pig got named "Chicken" in our attempt to separate feelings, fun, and fantasy.

I honestly didn't know what to do with Chicken. The kids became the absolute experts. I simply watched the pig grow as I drove back and forth, back and forth, and back and forth to the local feed store. (Note: This is not a typo; I think I was hired as a delivery driver for our pig's on-demand takeout needs. I am still looking for my tip, which he apparently lost in the mud.)

Once, I was asked if it could bathe in my bathtub, and as a good mom who lost her sanity, I said, "Sure. Let's go hog wild." I had absolutely no idea how loud a pig could squeal, especially when indoors in a tiny 1980s harvest-gold bathtub. His high-pitched squeaks resulted in excruciating pain between my eyes. I even worried that my mirrors would shatter because it sounded as if an opera singer had been asked to belt out the highest pitches.

As the months went on, the day finally came when the not-so-little-anymore pig moved from the garage space into the yard and grew larger and larger. The idea that an animal goes happily from fifty pounds to more than two hundred in less than four months was mind-blowing. From the start of the animal project, we always knew he would be sold off as the children learned about raising and tending to livestock.

The show-and-sell time rolled around, and I found myself wondering what life would feel like without a pig. My next "ah-ha moment" came when I learned about the *default option*—something I hadn't quite been fully briefed on. Despite all the slop, bagged food, and chocolate milk his devoted farmers (that's us) fed him, Chicken didn't make the required weight for the sale groups. Yes, you read that correctly. Apparently, I hadn't driven back and forth to the fairgrounds enough, because our hulking hog failed to hit the tonnage goal.

You guessed it: The pig stayed home.

We made it through sunny April, then May's relentless rain, and into the thick heat of June and July. While Chicken didn't smell quite as awful as I had expected, his stall still needed regular tending—fresh hay turned into the muddy trenches his snout had carved while searching for earthworms. He was a gentle soul, surprisingly playful, especially after he acquired a giant green ball he pushed around like a toddler at recess. Still, I couldn't help remembering that those jaws could crunch through bone if he wanted to.

So far, so good.

When I stepped into his pen, all 215-plus pounds of him would trot over to gnaw on my boots, nudging me like he's daring me to take a tumble into the mud. Luckily, we discovered his *kryptonite* by accident when he was a piglet.

One day, my daughter called in a panic: "Mom! I think the pig is dead! I've already called one of the local farmers!"

Oh no. We'd fed him, watered him, kept him warm, loved him—what could we have done wrong? Turns out, nothing. What we didn't know then was that pigs *love* belly rubs. Scratch their tummies with the back of a fork or rake, and they'll flop over like fainting goats—legs up, eyes closed, perfectly still. To the untrained eye, they look completely gone.

Now, at over two hundred pounds, Chicken doesn't exactly

"flop" gracefully. He collapses like a bloated ottoman tipping over in slow motion.

Just the other day, I was in his enclosure again. He started nudging me, so I picked up my shovel and thought, *All right, big guy, let's see what you've got.* I began scratching his side gently, brushing the mud from his ears, and—sure enough—*timber!* Down he went, flat on his back, sending a splash of mud flying like a belly flop at a pool party.

Thirty seconds later, my husband rolled up on the tractor, only to find me standing over this giant pig, shovel in hand, grinning like a conquering hero. "If your coworkers could see you now," he laughed, "they'd probably call an emergency meeting."

He's not wrong. But this island girl can proudly say she's earned her *Mama Farmer* badge this year. I've mastered the art of "tickling the pig"—a secret farming skill no manual ever mentioned.

So, go forth and share this sacred knowledge: Sometimes life's best lessons come when you least expect them—like when you're standing ankle-deep in mud, giggling over a snoring, belly-up pig.

The Furry Dictator

Cashmere Hagbourne

When I was twelve, I lived with a tyrant. A four-legged, blue-eyed, foot-slapping tyrant named Baozi—my Chinese Siamese cat.

Now, most cats knock things off tables for fun or casually ignore your existence until mealtime. Not Baozi. He had one mission in life: to keep me in bed. Every morning, without fail, the moment I dared move a toe beyond the safety of my blanket fortress—*SWIPE!* His little ninja paw would smack my foot like I'd just insulted his entire feline ancestry.

I'd be lying there, thinking, *Today's the day. I'll be faster than him.* I'd inch one leg toward the edge, barely a whisper of motion, and WHAP! Out of nowhere—paw to ankle. It was like living with a fluffy prison warden who specialized in foot-based violence.

I tried everything. I'd dangle decoy socks. I threw treats like grenades to lure him away. I even once whispered, "I'm going to the kitchen ... for *tuna*," hoping to distract him with lies. Nothing worked. Baozi would just stare at me like, *Try it, punk. Make my whiskers twitch.*

At one point, I truly believed he was psychic. Or a wizard. Or some ancient guardian assigned to make sure I never attended school again. I wasn't sure if he loved me or just hated mornings.

Then one day, everything changed. I caught him rolling around on the floor like he was auditioning for *So You Think You Can Dance: Cat Edition*. What was his secret sauce? Catnip. Apparently, it was his kryptonite.

That night, I launched Operation Get-Out-of-Bed. I sprinkled a small pinch of catnip near the end of the bed like I was casting a potion. Baozi strutted over, sniffed it once, and within seconds, he was on his back, eyes glassy, legs twitching in bliss. The heavens opened. Angels sang. I swung both legs out of bed—**freedom**.

From then on, every morning became a covert mission. I kept a stash of catnip in my nightstand like some kind of feline drug dealer. A little sprinkle here, a tiny pinch there. Baozi would drift off into his dreamland while I tiptoed away like a victorious ninja.

Some people trained their cats to sit. Others taught them to fetch. I drugged mine to stop him from assaulting my feet. That's childhood, right?

But looking back, I kind of miss it. Baozi didn't want me to leave because he liked me there—warm, cozy, predictable. In his weird, slightly aggressive way, he was showing love. Violent, toe-slapping love.

He's gone now, but I'll never forget those mornings—me, a sleepy middle schooler, and him, the furry dictator of my bed. And thanks to him, I learned two things: Never underestimate a cat and always keep a backup bag of catnip—just in case.

Princess and the B

Liz Sheahan

My first baby, Nickolas, loved to play with my bangs while I was nursing him. In fact, it quickly became something he relied on—if I didn't bend over for him to tangle his little fingers in the hair, he would fuss—something NO new mother wants. While very endearing, it led to my getting a very stiff neck.

So, I hunted through the many gifts we'd received which had been lovingly placed on the shelves and in the drawers of his nursery, looking for something I could transfer this habit to. The perfect solution was a lightweight woven cotton baby blanket, with strands of blue, yellow, pink, and white that led to fringe around all four edges.

The next feeding, I put the blanket up over my shoulder and led my son's chubby little digits to that soft fringe, and it worked like magic—I could hold my head upright and had a very content little guy. I was brilliant!

As Nickolas grew bigger, that blanket was never far away. While being read to or laying down to sleep, tugging on the fringe brought him great calm.

As he began to walk and talk, the blanket remained his favorite possession, getting increasingly ragged as time went on. He named it

B, and when he walked into a room and saw one of the strands that had come loose from B lying on the carpet, he'd exclaim with glee, "It's a B hair!"

His grandma sewed it up once, trying to hold it together better, to no avail. It eventually became so thin, B crumbled into a few different pieces—each as much adored as the other, so we left a small piece at each grandparent's home, in case we forgot to bring it on one of Nickolas's overnight stays. Even the main piece we kept at home was quite small after shedding so many of its "hairs" from all the handling and love.

When Nickolas was five, we got a collie puppy named Princess. We all loved our new family member very much—she was cuddly, playful, and well-behaved for a puppy.

One evening, we'd gone out for a quick dinner. Princess was proving to be quite trustworthy and wasn't wetting in the house anymore, so we left her loose in the house while we went to the local fast-food restaurant.

As we arrived home, dusk was setting in. Nickolas was the first to go into the living room, where he saw something unusual on the floor. Without the lights on yet, he put his face down close to the unknown object. "Oh my gosh!" he screamed as he ran out of the room, "It's a dead rat!"

I bolted over to see what he had seen and immediately knew that it was NOT a dead rat, but rather his small remaining piece of B that was tangled in a tubular shape and very slimy. The colored strings were evident to my mama-trained eyes. Clearly, Princess had decided to eat that delicious piece of fabric that smelled of her boy Nickolas, and she'd thrown it up right there on the living room carpet while we were out.

I knew this child was not going to settle down to bed that night without his beloved B, so what was I to do?

Being a calculating parent, I chose not to tell him what the object was (although I did tell him it was not a dead rat so he wouldn't be afraid). I quickly put the slimy cylindrical wad in a bucket of bleach and water, then washed and dried it before bedtime.

I must add that while that was the first time Princess ate and regurgitated B, it was not the last. I can't tell you how many times I bleached and washed that little comfort cloth, and, frankly, I'm not sure Nickolas, now a grown man, knows about it to this day.

Cat on an Ice-Cold Rock

Maggie van Galen

It was a cold New England night. The kind of cold that seeps into your bones. The temperature was well below freezing, but the sky was clear and the wind quiet. DiceK, our rescue kitty, phonetically named after the Boston Red Sox pitcher, Daisuke Matsuzaka, always had an adventurous spirit, but on this occasion had been out on his last run for a little too long.

Standing on the back deck, admiring the stars, I shook the bag of treats to encourage his return. A trick that usually worked. In the distance, a familiar meow called out. I trained my ear on the direction it came from. It was definitely DiceK. Donning a parka, boots, and the other winter accoutrements, I set off in search of the call. Down the driveway, left onto the street, and fifty yards further, there he was ... just on the other side of a four-foot-tall, chain-link fence.

Sitting in the tall grass, with his coat that matched the night sky and yellow eyes wide, he looked at me and cried.

"Hey, buddy," I said, "it's time to come home." I tried to reach him through the fence, to no avail. He didn't move. He was either hurt or trapped.

Enlisting the help of my husband, the rescue mission began. It's important to understand that the fence in question separates the road from a "conservation area" or *the bog*, as we call it. It's thick with vines and fallen trees, with swamp-like terrain. All sorts of critters call it home or use it as their nightly hunting ground, including coyotes and foxes. DiceK frequented the location, taking in the local scenery throughout every season.

In full bushwhacker mode, my hubby began the trek, with me holding a flashlight to guide his way. DiceK let out a grateful "*meowwww*" upon seeing us return. By then, it was close to midnight, and the temperature had dropped even further. Cold and shivering, our kitty just looked up at us, but still wasn't moving.

After further inspection, we saw that his beautiful, fluffy tail was frozen entirely to a small boulder ... from bum to tip! There was no way to separate the two. We decided the best course of action was to carry both the cat and the rock back to the house. The return journey was precarious and nerve-racking to say the least. Keep in mind the jungle-like environment, plus my husband was now carrying twenty pounds of kitty and stone. He had to go slowly and use extreme caution. If DiceK jumped or they slipped, DiceK might be injured or tear his tail off completely.

Led by torchlight and the moon's beam, we made our way back to the house, my husband's soothing tone constantly reassuring DiceK. Slow and steady.

After what seemed like hours (probably more like thirty minutes), we were back inside. Wrapped in a blanket and still being held, we soaked DiceK's tail in a large bowl of warm water. His fur slowly separated from the rock.

After several treats and a thorough once-over, DiceK snuggled into our bed between us and drifted off into a cozy slumber. He was home, warm, and safe!

Nearly fifteen years later, DiceK still ventures out, not so far anymore, is always home by ten, and sleeps between us every night!

Chicken, Ungifted

Dot Suggett

One day, at the end of a visit to a West African village, I was gifted a chicken. Clucks, squawks, and flying feathers enlivened our drive home. Our coworker, Kia, an experienced chicken wrangler, held onto the bird's feet, which were tied together with a strip of cloth.

My husband, Colin, looked with disfavor on this noisy, feathered intruder, but I liked my new pet. Each morning, I walked around the small house that served as our office. The ground was rocky and uneven, with sparse vegetation. I would carefully walk back and forth on the irregular surface until I found it: the daily egg laid by my pet chicken.

Chickie was not gifted with a motherly instinct; the egg would be laid haphazardly in the open, unprotected and forgotten. Sometimes an egg would be deposited beside the cooking hut, sometimes behind the main building, and just as often in a wide-open area of the yard. Each morning, when we drove the truck through the entrance gate, I checked the parking area to ensure that there would be no resulting scrambled eggs. It was like an extremely limited Easter egg hunt, every day! And I had no competition because my husband had no interest in either chicken or egg. Chickie's indifference to her potential offspring freed me from any guilt associated with my daily fried egg breakfast.

Despite her parental failings, I was fond of my chicken. I asked my national coworker, Kia, for advice: "What do I feed a chicken? I've never had one before."

Kia was incredulous—everyone knew how to raise chickens! Nevertheless, he patiently explained where I could buy bran and other feed in the local market. I was a responsible chicken mom. I provided her with kitchen scraps—she loved leftover spaghetti. Scratch at the dry and rocky soil all she would, she would never uncover earthworms. Spaghetti was as close as she would get to such tasty invertebrates, and I'm not sure her chicken brain knew the difference. I bought feed and kept a clean water bowl for her.

I greeted her with kind words, "How are you today, Chickie? Have you left a nice egg for me?"

My chicken, noncommittal, simply replied, "Cluck." Although my husband was not impressed with this barnyard intruder, I liked my chicken, and I enjoyed my daily egg.

Then my chicken gift disappeared.

Calling, "Here Chickie, Chickie, Chickie!" produced no results, to no one's great surprise. *Where was my chicken?* Such gifts were rare for us, and I had valued the unexpected but generous token of appreciation embodied in my little feathered friend. I gave up on the search after several days of finding neither chicken nor egg. "Maybe she was lonely. She must have found a way out," I lamented. I imagined her enjoying freedom with a flock of feral poultry. I felt like I had failed as a chicken mom.

Weeks later, an African neighbor, exuding irritation, came to our gate to complain about my chicken. "Come, come!" she snapped imperiously.

Accompanied by my coworker, Kia, I walked down the dusty path through a field of green sprouting corn adjacent to our office. We followed my neighbor's agitated figure as she stomped her way back to her house. She led us to a fenced-in corner of her yard where a dozen hens pecked and flapped on the ground beside a raised, straw-filled platform. Reaching into the nest area, she seized an egg and complained angrily, "Look! Its eggs don't hatch. It doesn't sit on them."

I had trouble following her dialect of the indigenous language I was learning, but I got the gist of her message. I tried in vain to recognize my pet among the squawking white poultry. Sadly, it seemed that Chickie had as much trouble recognizing me. If I had expected her to flutter over to me in instant recognition and relief, I was disappointed.

We stood in a potpourri of dirt, chicken feed, feathers, and droppings, while my neighbor continued to brandish the egg before me, all the while complaining bitterly. To my chagrin, she peeled the eggshell to reveal a dead chick curled up inside the egg, its yellow fluff plastered wetly against the tiny cold corpse.

My empty stomach lurched. Without my chicken's daily offering for the last month, I had not indulged in my favorite breakfast of a baguette with a yolky fried egg. The chick cadaver before me was undeniably my least favorite presentation of a morning egg.

I struggled to find the right words. "Um, why do you have my chicken?" I wanted to ask. I looked to Kia for help, but he was stone-faced. Being by nature conflict-averse, he knew that this woman was not going to be easily appeased. Seeking clarity, I settled on asking, "Who does this chicken belong to?"

She bristled with offense, appalled at my lack of appreciation. "I have been taking care of your chicken, and it isn't producing chicks." Her free hand gesticulated in the direction of the hens, and I finally saw her; Chickie was recognizable by the bright cloth strip we had left attached to her leg.

Mentally scrolling through other cross-cultural interactions, I tried to discern if this was a standard cultural practice. I came up empty. I needed some data. I looked to Kia, but he did not enlighten me on whether this behavior was normal.

However, he did fill in more information. "She has been feeding your chicken. The chicken lays eggs, but there are no chicks. She wants you to do something about it."

That helped to explain her irritation. But I was still mystified. Had I asked her to feed my chicken? No. Had she informed me about this chicken foster care scheme? No. Was it really okay to keep my chicken's eggs for herself? Well ... maybe? Of course, I couldn't articulate all this in her language. I appealed to Kia, speaking in French, "So, the idea was that she could take my chicken without telling me, feed it, raise the chicks for herself, and deprive me of my daily egg. Do I have this right?"

Kia was as noncommittal as my chicken. He replied with an expressive Gallic shrug. Smart move, Kia. You have to live in this neighborhood.

So, how was I supposed to navigate such a cultural conundrum? I sadly acknowledged that this impasse required a sacrifice on my part. I knew I couldn't reclaim Chickie. The scenario would only repeat itself. Looking sadly at my dear but non-maternal chicken, I sighed with resignation and accepted my eggless future. I asked Kia to translate my winner-take-all solution: "I'll tell you what. Let's give the lady the feed I bought and let her keep the chicken." I may have been assigning my feathered friend to a future involving intimate interaction with a stew pot, but this situation was beyond my cross-cultural navigation skills.

Colin would regret that Chickie ended up in the neighbor's peanut sauce and not ours, but I couldn't share his sentiment. I had enjoyed a short but memorable interval with my unanticipated pet chicken. I knew my husband would be relieved to once again have the freedom to drive into the yard and park, without my frenzied efforts to keep Chickie in the yard and rescue any vulnerable eggs. I admit, a subtle flicker of relief eased my mind. I was free of the heavy responsibility and distraction of chicken parenting. I did not seek a replacement feathered pet. In future village visits, Colin and I rushed our exit to dodge any potential chicken gifts.

Looking back along the dirt path to my neighbor's chicken-filled yard, I caught a last glimpse of my pet. I whispered a quiet farewell: "Goodbye, chicken gift. Goodbye, eggs."

"Cluck."

Lizards, Turtles, and Frogs, Oh My!

Cynthia Schulz

Our family is petless, but not for lack of trying.

I always thought having a pet would be good for our four kids—Big Brother, Big Sister, Little Sister, and Baby Boy. Most especially for Big Sister, the sibling with special needs.

Simba the cat was our first attempt. We took her to the vet, who lifted her tail and declared, "Simba is a Himba." Our first surprise.

Then, a year later, when allergy-prone Little Sister developed asthma, Simba had to move to our cousin's house for the next twenty-two years.

At least we saw him on holidays!

Each Thanksgiving Day, the kids would dart past a houseful of relatives in search of Simba, who was very good at hiding. But he was no match for Big Brother, who was very good at finding him in his favorite spot behind the clothes dryer in Auntie's laundry room. And the family reunion was on!

Since all critters with fur were out of the question for us, we had to get creative. On a vacation in Florida, the kids captured a tiny yard lizard and kept it alive by feeding it bugs and water. "Please, please, please," begged Baby Brother, "can we take Lizzy home with us?"

I was pretty sure on our twenty-hour drive back to Ohio, Lizzy wouldn't make it to Georgia, so I said yes.

Lizzy lived her full two-year lifespan in Ohio in the comfort of her tricked-out glass habitat, with a steady diet of freeze-dried flies and water, treated occasionally to a live ant or spider. The kids loved showing her off to their friends, especially each time she outgrew and shed her skin.

After Lizzy, I thought we were done. Until Big Brother came home from college with a gigantic fish tank fully stocked, something he knew I would not want in my house. To soften me up, he oh-so-thoughtfully bought Big Sister with special needs her very own baby turtle the size of a quarter to plop in, making it impossible for me to kick the aquarium to the curb.

We were stuck with a turtle in a fish tank in the foyer.

She named her new turtle Bee Bop and waved to him every day on her way in and out the front door. Soon, he was the size of a hockey puck, the largest creature in our underwater menagerie.

When Bee Bop appeared lethargic one day, I became worried about the pet we'd all become attached to. I took him an hour's drive to a turtle vet, waited until they called for "Bee Bop's family," and felt pretty guilty when they pronounced him malnourished.

Who knew turtles could not live on fish food alone?

Yes, of course, please pump him with nutrients, was my decision. A hundred dollars later, we were on our way home.

"You spent how much?!" my husband gasped. "You should've gone to the store and bought another turtle for ten bucks," he said heartlessly.

I set newly invigorated Bee Bop back onto his lily pad, where he performed a swan dive to the bottom of the tank—and expired.

Oh my. How to tell the kids? For three of them, it was easy because they were unfazed. But how would Big Sister with special needs handle the bad news?

Ever so tenderly, we explained that Bee Bop went to turtle

heaven. With eyes wide open, she snapped, "That's it. He's gone." Apparently, no one cared a hoot about our turtle, besides me.

For closure, we buried Bee Bop in a small box under a rock in our front yard. I tried to say a little prayer but was drowned out by a backdrop of irreverent teenagers rolling their eyes, cracking jokes, stifling laughter, and groaning, "This is ridiculous, Mom. Can we go now?"

Just when I thought we were done trying out pets, those same kids turned around and gave their sister two dwarf frogs in a Frog-O-Sphere for Christmas. We named them Sunday and Thursday because those were the days we fed them their pellets.

I wasn't sad when they finally died several years later, until those blasted kids went out and bought her two more! We named these Monday and Friday. They're finally gone now, too.

After trial and mostly error, alas, we've hit on the perfect pet for Big Sister. Snickerdoodle is her beloved, weighted stuffed bulldog with sensory powers who sits on her lap, sleeps with her at night, and goes on vacations with us. Getting the plushy through TSA at the airport can be tricky, but he's low-maintenance otherwise.

The circular conversation between them goes like this: "Are you a good boy? You're a good boy! Are you my buddy? You're my buddy! Miss me? I missed you! Love me? I love you!"

Over time, Snickerdoodle tends to develop rips and tatters and lose his stuffing. That's when we treat him to a spa day. He comes home looking and smelling brand new (wink wink)!

He's a keeper!

The Day a Dog Saved Us
(An Irish Road Trip Tale)
Jen Kline Clark

BACK IN 2001, RIGHT AFTER SEPTEMBER 11, MY HUSBAND, Patrick, and I found a great deal for a flight to Ireland, a rental car, and seven nights in bed and breakfasts. We landed on the west coast and had seven days to get to the east coast. We were newly married, broke, and looking for adventure. So, Ireland it was!

This was our first time driving in Europe. Left side of the road, right side of the car, all of it is (literally) foreign to us, and we are fumbling every inch. And in Ireland, where straight roads apparently do not exist, every day felt like a daily game of "will we survive this turn?"

Fast forward to one of our last mornings. It was misty and magical, and we're cruising into yet another quiet little town: church, post office, pub—the usual. But as we pull into town, *bam*—flat tire. Cue the rain, cue us pulling over.

Now here's the thing: The tools to change the tire are under all our luggage. We're on the side of the road, unpacking like mad, trying to act like we know what we're doing. And while we're mid-chaos, this dog appears. Just ... shows up. Sits a few feet away. Watching.

Not barking, not begging. Just observing us like we were the morning's entertainment.

We tried everything to remove that tire. But the bolts were clearly tightened by some kind of mechanical god. There was no way we could have gotten that thing off with only our human strength.

We were soaked, stuck, and starting to panic a little. Meanwhile, the dog—still quiet—gets up and walks off.

We thought nothing of it. We were still stuck in problem-solving mode.

But five minutes later? The dog returned—with *two burly Irishmen* in tow.

They came over, chuckling as we explained the situation. Turned out, the whole town was at church ... except these two, who had skipped the service to hang out in their garage with a couple of beers. The dog had walked in, stared at them, and trotted out like, "*Come on, lads. Tourists need help.*"

They followed him, found us, and, in less than five minutes, they got the tire off, the spare on, and our bags repacked. They even invited us for a drink at their garage—but we were too stunned and soggy to take them up on it.

They refused our money. So, we hugged the dog instead.

And that was how a random Irish dog became the unexpected hero of our Irish road trip.

A New Leash on Life

Tassie Kalas

The best thing I did after my divorce was get a dog. I didn't realize how empty my home was until Archie, a lovable and huggable mini goldendoodle, filled it with love. Faithful and loyal, he was everything my ex-husband was not.

After a long day, I could count on him to greet me at the door with a wagging tail and a happy smile. My confidant and companion, he'd watch rom-coms with me curled up on the sofa and gently awaken me with a lick on the face if I dozed off during the juicy parts. His acute hearing alerted me to danger (or DoorDash) long before my Ring doorbell did, and his surprisingly ferocious bark scared off solicitors, so I didn't have to. He guarded my heart and home, keeping me feeling safe and secure. After years of living with drama and chaos, I welcomed the peaceful haven my home had become.

Our relationship was a fetch made in heaven—until we walked outside. Easygoing and relaxed for twenty-three hours of the day, the minute Archie spotted me putting on my running shoes, his fluffy ears would shoot straight up. All it took was for him to get a glimpse of the blue leash in my hand, and he'd explode into a bubbly ball of energy, bouncing up as high as my shoulders, eager to perform the one job he'd been born to do: Protect Mom at all costs. No amount of begging, training, or Trader Joe's beef rolls for dogs could convince him otherwise.

We'd barely make it out the front door when he'd stiffen and freeze, a low, menacing growl vibrating through his thirty-five-pound body. "It's just a leaf, Archie." I tried to reason with him. "The squirrel's not hurting us. That's a Christmas decoration, not a real reindeer!" Despite my reassurances, he'd march down the street ahead of me, his long ears whipping from left to right as he scouted out the treacherous path ahead.

I tried to take him for walks when I knew there'd be fewer neighbors out, when the kids were in school and the street was quiet. One unsuspecting FedEx deliveryman learned the hard way not to stop and chat. "Down, Archie!" I swallowed whatever pride I had left after my divorce. "Give the nice man his clipboard back."

Despite my precautions, an encounter was inevitable. It was a crisp, cool, beautiful Houston winter day, and I was looking forward to a peaceful walk in the sun with my best boy. Packing my crossbody with treats and poopy bags, I selected my favorite playlist on my phone, then clipped the leash onto Archie's collar. Sharing my excitement, he burst out the door, pulling me after him. We circled the block without incident. Emboldened by his good behavior, I decided to brave a quick trip to the park. I glanced down at his shining eyes, and my heart welled with emotion. He was such a good boy. What could possibly go wrong?

I spied the man before Archie did. Tall in stature with a serious look on his face, he strode towards us, a well-behaved goldendoodle, wearing a fetching pink bow prancing by his side. I tugged Archie's leash and pulled him off the sidewalk to clear the path so the two could pass.

"Look, Archie!" I gestured wildly at an empty water bottle in the grass to distract him, but his brown eyes zeroed in on the doodle drawing closer. A soft growl grumbled in his chest. "Wanna chase some squirrels? How about a tasty treat?" I dug frantically in my bag, searching for a sweet potato snack as the pair grew nearer.

I had just gotten my fingers on a tiny morsel when Archie, drooling from the mouth, lunged at the startled doodle, and my bag went flying through the air. "Archie, down!" I commanded in my most threatening, angry mom voice, but the spawn of Cujo ignored me, redirecting his attention instead to the crotch of the man's dress pants. I watched in horror as my sweet, loving indoor dog buried his nose between the poor man's legs, sniffing and nuzzling him like he had sausage sticks stashed in his pockets. "I'm so sorry!" I called out to the stranger who stared stoically ahead as man's best friend continued the degrading assault. My face grew hot from embarrassment as I fought to control my dog with one hand and stooped to pick up my belongings with the other: some stray dollar bills, breath mints in case I met a nice man on my walk, and pepper spray in case I met a bad one. I pulled Archie down the sidewalk as he barked in protest.

Fuming, I stomped to the park, the perfect day turning as dark as my mood. I should have never left my neighborhood. I should have never left my house. I should have never gotten a dog. As if sensing my disapproval, Archie fell silent and walked softly by my side, the leash loose between us.

I led us to a park bench and collapsed onto the cold iron seat; my shoulders slumped in defeat. An icon of innocence, Archie plopped down in the grass at my feet, gazed up at me with puppy dog eyes, and tilted his head, his monogrammed bandanna fluttering in the wind. Despite myself, a small smile curled on my lips, and I searched for my phone so I could take a selfie of this Instagram moment. Archie was being a dog, after all. It wasn't his fault that he got a little excited when an attractive doodle came along. It wasn't his fault; he was just trying to protect me from a strange man.

I canvassed my bag for my phone, growing more frantic by the second. Dumping the contents onto the bench beside me, I took a quick inventory and glared at the furry ball of fluff at my feet. "Archie!" I cried. "This is all your fault!"

Jumping up, I retraced my steps along the path, dragging the dazed doodle behind me. My phone could have fallen out anywhere. I thought of the thousands of prized photos it contained, the unread emails, the apps I never thought I'd need that now I couldn't live without. I quickened my step; eyes peeled to the ground. Like a hysterical mother whose teen had missed curfew, I imagined the worst—my phone smashed to bits and dead on the side of the road, a victim of a hit and run, or kidnapped and sold into text trafficking.

A low growl rumbled in Archie's throat, and his sudden stop made me look up. In the distance, I could barely discern a person waving wildly, and my heart skipped a beat. Had a friendly neighbor found my phone? I hurried forward, Archie growing more agitated with every step. As we got closer, I recognized the man from the trail, clutching my phone, waving me down as if he were trying to land a plane, his prissy sidekick planted primly by his side. My face reddened at the memory of our last encounter, and I yanked the leash firmly to rein in my reckless dog.

"Thank you!" I cried. "You found my phone!" I reached out to take it from him, but before we could make contact, Archie howled in protest.

The man's eyes widened, and his other hand flew down to protect his still-damp crotch.

"Archie, sit!" I commanded. "Stay!" I stretched my hand out again, more slowly this time, barely brushing my fingertips on the edge of the phone when Archie went ballistic, barking like a banshee.

"I'm sorry," I repeated for the tenth time that day as I struggled to grip the leash tighter. "He's harmless. Really. Wouldn't hurt a ..." I glanced at the man's soggy crotch and blushed. "Fly."

I gave Tall, Dark, and Handsome my brightest smile when, before I could stop him, Archie lunged, running circles around us, forcing us into an awkward group hug, his leash tying me, the speechless dog owner, and his yelping pup into one neat package. I could feel the man's breath, indignant and hot, on my bare neck as my devilish doodle wrapped us tighter and tighter together in a steamy embrace.

It was the closest I'd come to a man since my divorce.

I struggled to turn my body away, but that only made it worse. The four of us were trapped on a disastrous double date, and I hadn't even gotten a steak dinner out of the whole ordeal. "Maybe we were destined to meet this way," I murmured into the man's ear, but true to character, he remained silent.

In the end, Archie was one lucky dog. Daisy, the diva doodle, finally submitted to his irresistible charm. Rolling onto her back, she kicked her perfectly groomed legs in the air and invited my shameless hound to take a sniff. It was just the distraction we needed.

My dog-walking date, clearly moved by this puppy display of affection, raised his eyebrows and shot me a fetching look.

"Don't get any ideas," I said to him as I untangled myself, adjusted my clothes, and made sure my cell phone was zipped safely inside my bag. "I'm not that kind of girl."

As if on cue, Archie appeared by my side, tail wagging, oblivious to the drama his matchmaking had put me through. It was dinner time; he was ready to escort me home, and I was eager to get there. Despite his disgraceful behavior, I still found him hard to resist. Besides, I wasn't ready to be tied down, anyway.

I tossed my hair and the two of us strutted off into the sunset. After all, Archie and I had an agreement. He didn't mind my tugging on his leash, and I didn't mind him pulling on my heart.

Showing off the Neighbors

Liz Sheahan

We were living in a unique, very rural-esque area of San Diego County. While it was just a short drive in any direction to the busy streets and commerce of town, the winding roads around our home wrapped around cool little hobby farms, giving us the feel of living in the country. We woke to roosters crowing, watched our neighbors stroll by on horseback, and held our breath as coyotes ran through the yard.

One of my favorite walks took me past a little farm with a dozen or more goats—I absolutely loved visiting them. Oftentimes, the curious little herd would come right up to the fence to greet me. I'd stop and talk to them before moving up on the road to a trailhead that took me through the rolling hills. The goats were often very playful and silly, which brought me great joy.

One weekend, when my son Joe was home from college, I chose to take him on that walk so I could show him my favorite neighbors—the goats.

Joe is a very tall, talkative guy. As we were about fifty yards from the goat pen, I told him, "Good! The goats are out. I want you to see them."

As we both looked ahead toward the herd, one of the taller goats stretched its neck, lifting its head high above the others around it to get a good look at us. Then he bleated alarmingly, which sounded exactly like he was saying, "Oh, my God!"

I couldn't believe what I heard and saw. Wide-eyed, I turned to Joey, who was like my mirror image. He witnessed the very same thing. We burst into laughter!

When we looked back at the goats, the entire herd was running away from us, toward their shelter.

Perhaps he was intimidated by Joey's height or low voice, or maybe it was just one of those days. We'll never know, but it has given us years of laughter as we look at each other wide-eyed and exclaim, "Oh, my God!" in our finest goat imitation.

Boys of a Feather

Jennifer D. Munro

At fifteen, my son, the Junior Terrorist, stands six-foot-two and still climbing. Rising to a similar height is JT's Best Bird-watching Friend, Biff. "We do not bird*watch*, Mom. We *bird*," JT corrects me whenever I once again misrepresent his true life calling—as if I have confused Ping-Pong for Wimbledon.

Their shoes keep climbing higher in the double digits, and they lumber along, lanky yet hulking, their clothes baggy. The bird-watching equipment they lug around enlarges them further: binoculars and cameras and scopes and tripods, backpacks and water bottles and field guides and notebooks. Their lunches they've likely forgotten on the kitchen counter. They are adorable—largely because I glimpse them briefly in full birding plumage before they head off for hours by themselves somewhere far, far away, leaving me in a quiet house.

At least for now, they're outside, their curiosities inexplicably piqued by birds rather than by what's on the other side of restricted computer web pages; this gives me hope, as well as unrestricted access to my hidden chocolate stash while they're gone.

Recently, my husband, Richard, and JT were supposed to pick

up Biff on the way to Richard's early morning meeting across town so the two teens could bird at a Birding Hotspot nearby. But when Richard and JT got to Biff's house, Biff wasn't there. Biff's brother said that Biff had walked to the bus stop. He'd forgotten he was getting a ride.

Richard and JT drove to the bus stop. Biff wasn't there, either.

"I've got to get to my meeting on time," Richard told JT. They couldn't spend more time looking for Biff.

As they drove away, they saw Biff sprinting back to his house, his equipment banging against him, looking like a paparazzo gunning for a Beyoncé candid, not a Gadwall glimpse.

Richard, already late and heading down a busy street in the opposite direction, couldn't stop and turn around.

Biff called me at home, asking for JT's phone number, since Biff had lost his phone, and his mom's borrowed phone didn't have JT's number programmed into it. But JT didn't have his phone with him that morning—too much to carry!—though bringing it had been (ahem) suggested to him. So, there was no way to reach him. (JT has since lost his phone, too.)

The two towering teenage birders, as obvious as Big Bird wandering the suburbs, never did find each other that morning. As Biff's mom said to me later, there was a lesson for them to be learned here. (Spoiler: No lesson was learned.)

Studies show that the benefits of being in nature include helping to improve the symptoms of ADHD. Imagine what this pair would be like *without* bird-watching.

Once, after we left a park where I'd driven them to bird, Biff left his backpack in the parking lot, right behind my back tire.

When I chaperoned them to an island to bird, Biff realized as the ferry home loaded that he'd left his scope where we'd eaten lunch. "You'd better run fast and go get it," I said. If we didn't make this ferry, we could be stuck on the island (with no running water, electricity, or services) for hours. I've never seen a teenager run so fast in response to an adult directive in my life. He understood that I was fully prepared to leave him behind in order to return to a civilized bathroom.

Last weekend, they went on their third annual Big Day, where enthusiasts around the globe count as many bird species as they can on the same day. Each year, for Biff's birthday, Biff's mom drives them vast distances, from before sunup to well after sundown—because she's nice and obviously insane. In JT's recent unfortunate flirtation with the full range of English vocabulary, it's because I'm an "a$$hole," while she's "pretty cool."

They counted 132 bird species in a single day. Not 132 species like pelicans, huge and recognizable by four-year-old city dwellers. No: 132 types of itty-bitty brown thingamajigs flitting far away in overgrown brown fields or up high in the branches of brown trees. Birds secreted in forests at midnight. Birds burrowing in elusive cliffs.

It's a mystery to me. These two sometimes *cannot even manage to find each other*—two tall teenage boy birders who stick out in our culture like, well, two tall teenage boy birders—yet they can spot and identify oodles of frenetic specks on the horizon. In fact, they don't even need to see the specks to identify them: They can identify them by bird calls, flight pattern, or some other elusive trait. Let's call the boys enthusiastically intuitive rather than jumping-the-gun know-it-alls.

JT and I have conversations like this:

Me: "I saw this bird on a flowering cherry yesterday that—"

JT: "Goldfinch."

Me: "But maybe—"

JT: "Nope, couldn't be. Those are migrating"

Me: "But it—"

JT: "Lesser Goldfinch."

And the thing is, I know that he is correct.

How do these two frenzied and frantic Globetrotter-sized bird chasers not scare the birds away? I can hear *both* sides of their phone conversations when JT is downstairs and two rooms over while they gab for hours. About birds.

Then there's the *PISHING*. No, this does not involve the grossness of the toilet bowl rim revealed by the perennially un-put-down toilet seat. When JT thinks he's seen a rare leucistic eiderwhatsit as we drive along, he yells for me stop, and leaps out of the car (sometimes waiting until I brake), going, "Psssshhhhh! Psssshhhhh! Pssssshhhhh!" In theory, the attempt to replicate bird language is to fool the bird that JT is another bird on a friendly tourist junket. As in, "I might *look* like an eighteen-wheeler compared to you, but, come on, would something that could crush you with its big toe mean you harm when it sounds like a ... um ... sparrow, sort of?"

Pishing sounds like no bird that I know of and more resembles a snake with a big secret. It strikes me as condescending to the birds, like in old Westerns where white guys try to communicate with Native Americans: "How. We come in peace." Yeah, right.

All *pishing* really accomplishes is scaring the birds away before I have a chance to see them, too.

And, as my birding teacher instructs, *pishing* distracts the birds from vital survival activities: trivial tasks like eating and defending territory. It depletes the energy they need to thrive. But try telling that to a teen who happens to know he's an expert at something.

I guarantee you that JT could list all 132 Big Day species off the top of his head, as well as where and when he saw them, down to the second. Yet after Big Day, JT scrawled a note: "Mom, where is the SD card for my camera?"

He'd written it on the back of his Spanish teacher's broken plea for help in getting JT to memorize the vocab and stop disrupting class.

How should I know where his SD card is, even if I knew what it was?

I pointed out to him that he'd missed the point of Big Day being a fundraiser for the Audubon Society. Folks pledge a dollar amount per bird. Think of the funds he could have raised with 132 sightings!

"I did not miss the memo!" he spat. "Birding's just Something We Do." I had profaned the sacred and holy with my suggestion of pairing birding with filthy lucre.

The boys fantasize about doing a Global Big Year. Imagine. Twelve months of *pishing* ... out of my earshot.

They might manage to see thousands of bird species—if they manage to locate their own plane.

The Chupacabra Chihuahua

Judi Harrington

Here's the thing: I'm a writer—not just in the "I have a blog" kind of way, but in the "people hire me for my way with words" sort of way. In certain circles—some far, some wide—I'm known for my linguistic finesse, encyclopedic recall of obscure facts, and gift for turning complexity into clarity. I am, in fact, the *coveted* trivia partner at school fundraisers and bar quizzes.

But when I get something wrong? I don't just miss the mark—I spectacularly detonate the target.

I'm not talking about a casual typo or a misplaced comma. No, I don't simply miss the mark when I get it wrong. I go down in a blaze of glory, taking logic, meaning, and sometimes my dignity with me.

Case in point: my first documented Malaprop Moment. It happened about ten years ago during the height of my Zumba phase with my dear friend Diane. (We were Real Housewives of Middlesex County, if you must know—less diamonds, more dry shampoo.) Diane, the overachiever of the two of us, also did Pilates at the same studio. She's a doctor, so she can justify these things as "wellness." I just needed the break from my household. Potato, potahto.

One day, Diane called to tell me she'd hurt herself at Pilates.

"I hurt my cervical spine," she said, sounding matter of fact.

"Oh, my goodness! That sounds *awful!*" I replied, cringing as my whole body tensed with sympathy.

"Well, it's always something," she sighed, "but I think I'll be okay."

A few nights later, we met for drinks, and Diane walked in wearing a neck brace.

"What's with the neck brace?" I asked.

"I *hurt my cervical spine*, remember?" she replied.

And that's when it hit me.

"*Oooohhhhhh*. You know when you hear one word and think of another? When you said, 'cervical spine,' I heard 'cervix.' And I've been wondering *how the hell you did that*."

"WHAT?" she gasped.

"I know! I mean, they're *very* different body parts."

"How can you be so smart and mix up those two things?"

"I have no idea. I'm talented, I guess."

We still laugh about that one. And even though I now have a firm grasp on the difference between a neck and a cervix, I've sworn off Pilates—just in case.

But of course, one Malaprop Moment does not a pattern make.

Yet, because I am an overachiever in all the wrong things, it wasn't long before another one came along—another scene, another slip, another chance for my brain to wander off script while my mouth confidently charges ahead. And yes, Diane was there for this one, too.

This time, the confusion involved not the human body ... but the animal kingdom.

And friends, let me say: If you thought the cervix thing was bad, *you haven't met Sallie yet.*

Diane and her family have always been dog people—like, *capital D* Dog People. When I met her, their beloved Dwight was nearing the end of his life. A dignified, geriatric gentleman, Dwight crossed the Rainbow Bridge shortly after.

Two months later, despite her dramatic pronouncement of "No more dogs!" Diane found herself unable to withstand the collective gloom of her household. She caved—of course she did—and on the Ides of March, no less, welcomed a new pup into the fold: Duddy.

Duddy was chaos incarnate, but we hardly had time to get attached before Sallie arrived and stole the spotlight—and the storyline.

Sallie's origin story was the kind you couldn't make up: Rescued from an alley in California by Diane's nephew and his wife, they named her Alley and gave her a new lease on life. That is, until they had a baby, and Alley bit the child. Suddenly, no one wanted the dog, and as Diane put it, "It was gonna be curtains for her."

Diane, never one to ignore a family plea (especially one accompanied by nephew-tears), stepped in. Alley moved across the country and was reborn as Sallie, named by Diane in what I can only assume was an attempt to redeem her past sins.

A few weeks later, Diane and I found ourselves, once again, waiting outside a music studio while our respective cherubs toiled away at piano lessons. As always, I asked after the latest in canine developments.

"So, how's it going with Sallie?"

Diane groaned. "She is a pure chupacabra. She's into everything. Wreaking havoc."

Now, "chupacabra" was a new one for me. But in context—disruptive, wild, hard to contain—I assumed it was a breed. One of those rare, spicy-sounding dogs you only hear about on NPR fundraisers or in Gwyneth Paltrow's gift guides.

Content with my application of deductive reasoning based on semantic cues (also: I was a tired mom and simply had no energy to press the matter further), I filed this tidbit of information away in my head: "Diane has a Mexican breed dog called a chupacabra."

The kids came bounding out of their lesson, and the conversation shifted. I didn't press for details. I was too busy navigating the logistics of post-piano chaos and mentally negotiating whether dinner could be cereal.

Days passed. Then weeks. Maybe months. And then, during a catch-up with our mutual friend Marie, the subject reappeared.

"So, Diane got a new dog, huh? What kind is it?" Marie asked.

I responded with the misplaced confidence of someone who *almost* knows something:

"I'm not totally sure, but Diane said she's a chupacabra, so I think it's a rare Mexican breed."

Marie raised an eyebrow. "That sounds exotic."

"Yes," I said, basking in the glow of my faux expertise. "Very exotic."

But then Marie and I were interrupted by children, spouses, or both, so the subject was ceremoniously dropped.

It wasn't until *much* later, as in *three years later*, that I learned the truth.

The chupacabra is not a breed.

It is a *demon*.

Specifically, a mythical creature rumored to suck the blood of livestock. A Latin American goat vampire. Not exactly a rescue-dog success story.

When I finally brought this up to Diane—still imagining Sallie as a scrappy desert-born mischief-maker with questionable lineage—I asked, "So what kind of dog is Sallie, really? You said she was a chupacabra. Is that a breed?"

Diane stared at me, stunned into silence. Then, blinking in disbelief, she replied, "A chupacabra is a *monster,* Judi. It's a thing that kills goats. It's not a *dog*. Why didn't you Google it?"

"Oh. Yeah. I guess I could have done that."

Sometimes I'm Judi 411—your reliable source, a font of knowledge, overflowing with facts, trivia, and just the right turn of phrase.

Other times, I'm Judi 404: Information Not Found. A walking, talking example of how contextual clues can lead even the sharpest minds astray.

In the end, I wasn't completely off base—Sallie was, in fact, a chihuahua. Or, as Diane described her: "A criminal I harbored for six years until she died on Joe's lap—*unbeknownst to him*—on February 24, 2020. She had the good sense to cut out before the Coronafest."

The end.

Or is it? Because with my track record ... there's always another Malaprop Moment waiting in the wings.

About the Authors

Renee Burns Lonner is a management consultant for television newsrooms and a licensed psychotherapist based in Los Angeles. During the pandemic, she shifted from professional writing to humor writing (and she is never going back!). Renee has published two books, *If You Give a Man a Tesla: A Parody* and *We're Sorry to Inform You That... YOUR FORTIES ARE OVER*, plus multiple essays that have been published by *Medium*, *LOL Comedy*, and Erma Bombeck Writers Workshop blog. Her *Forties* book won two awards, a Zibby and Storytrade. Learn more at reneelonner.com.

Glenda Ferguson's experiences as a junior high teacher came in handy when she performed stand-up comedy at the 2024 Erma Bombeck Writing Workshop. Glenda won first place for her photography at the 2025 Dogwood Festival but doesn't anticipate overexposure in that development. Glenda and her husband, Tim, live in southern Indiana, where their tabby cat, Scrappy, and the wildlife visitors cause daily animal mayhem.

January Gordon Ornellas is a humor writer whose work has appeared in the *LA Times, The Belladonna*, and *Chicken Soup for the Soul*. Her short story, "Play Nice," was a runner-up in the prestigious 2022 Erma Bombeck Writing Competition. January's collection of humorous essays, *My Above Average Colon and Other Midlife Adventures*, was published in 2023. When she's not writing for her blog, https://midlifebloomer.com/, she enjoys running, traveling, and spending time with her family.

Cashmere Hagbourne, MSW and (PhD Ed candidate) is a dynamic artist, author, and entrepreneur whose passion for creativity and community shines through everything he does. As director of business development at the Family Freedom Center, he empowers youth and local entrepreneurs to dream big, build boldly, and thrive sustainably—while also cultivating growth through a vibrant community garden. Creator of the uplifting children's book, *Afromations,* Cashmere inspires self-love, culture, and purpose everywhere he goes.

Ryan Hale writes across genres because he's never been good at staying in one lane. His *Blake Franklin Investigations* novels serve up Texas-sized mysteries where the good guys still wear white hats, and his *Wallingford Heights* stories bring history and small-town life to vivid, everyday detail. Under the names Anne LeCarrè and Sophia Everly, he turns his attention to love—its humor, heartbreak, and the hope that keeps us all going. A lifelong writer and restaurateur, he brings the same attention to flavor and detail to his fiction as he does to his Denton, Texas restaurant, 940's Kitchen & Cocktails. His stories are crafted for readers who believe good still triumphs, faith still guides, and love still redeems. Writing full-time for just under three years, Ryan is finding his lifelong love of storytelling very satisfying.

Judi Harrington is a writer, book coach, and storyteller who translates complex ideas into clear, compelling narratives. She specializes in writing for technical industries—including real estate, finance, and law—helping professionals sound human without losing their edge. Her work appears in anthologies, podcasts, and writing circles that celebrate humor, heart, and the occasional plot twist. Learn more about Judi's work and writing coaching at judi411.com.

Caroline Horwitz writes humor from Pittsburgh, where she lives with her husband, kids, and unimpressed cat. Her work has appeared in *McSweeney's*, *Points in Case*, *Weekly Humorist*, *The Belladonna Comedy*, *Slackjaw*, *Frazzled*, and other publications. You can read more at www.carolinehorwitzwriting.com.

Tassie Kalas writes about marriage, motherhood, dog hair, and divorce. Her book, *Yaya's Big Black Purse: Drama of a Greek Mama*, was a finalist in the Story Circle Network Gilda Book Award competition for humor. Her stories about growing up and growing older have appeared in *Chicken Soup for the Soul* and other anthologies. Through the bittersweet journey of life, she still believes in happily ever laughter—and hopes you do, too. Visit her at www.tassietypes.com.

Jen Kline Clark is a business reset strategist who helps brilliant, seasoned women entrepreneurs stop spinning their wheels and start hearing YES again. She's a storyteller, world wanderer, and mom of two, known for mixing bold clarity with big heart (and the occasional dog disaster). Whether she's untangling a client's offer or navigating a skunky situation at 4 a.m., Jen brings humor, grit, and serious strategy to the table—mostly from her home in Bucks County, PA.

Alice S. Marks was once the director of an early childhood center, and alongside her husband of sixty-one years, she raised four children in a home joyfully overrun with pets. Those wonderfully chaotic kid-and-critter years gifted her an endless supply of humorous material for her retirement life as a humor columnist, anthology contributor, and novelist. She has hybrid-published three Corpus Christi mysteries, and her latest book, *Shadows on the Moon* (2024), is an eco-fantasy set within an endangered commune inside the moon.

Kelly McKenzie is the author of the coming-of-age memoir, *Never, Never, Hardly Ever: A Mother/Daughter Story of Antiques* *and Antics*. It spills the tea on the secrets behind her type-A mother's successful antique shop and how they survived working together for over a decade. This quirk magnet also blogs at www.kellylmckenzie.com, and her stories have been published in several anthologies, including *Laugh Out Loud* and the *Chicken Soup for the Soul* series.

Amy Mullis writes and avoids wildlife in upstate South Carolina. Her home is full of animals (and family) who stopped to smell the bacon and found out she could whip up gravy like she's the love child of Indiana Jones and Gordon Ramsey. She has written for a smorgasbord of anthologies, the *Christian Science Monitor*, and *Sasee* magazine, and makes occasional guest appearances on her blog, Mind Over Mullis.

Jennifer D. Munro's prose has appeared in numerous journals and anthologies, including *The Bigger the Better the Tighter the Sweater: 21 Funny Women on Beauty and Body Image*; *Defenestration: a Literary Magazine Dedicated to Humor*; and *Raven Chronicles'* humor issue. She is a two-time Pushcart Prize nominee, a Top Ten Finalist in the Erma Bombeck Global Humor Competition, and a winner of the National Society of Newspaper Columnists blog contest (in the "blogs nobody reads" category).

Jennifer Priest Mitchell has written her way through life's hopes and headaches since she was a child in Ohio. She earned a BA from Capital University in Columbus and an MA from Arizona State University in Phoenix. Jennifer has published with *Chicken Soup for the Soul*, the *Mocking Owl Roost*, and many small publications. She loves traveling and hiking with her family and friends; she likes her day job with a Hospice organization; and she dreams of a career that consists entirely of writing (and publishing), fueled by hot chai tea and caramels all day, every day. Learn more at www.jenniferpriest-mitchell.com.

Robin Raniero Norris is a mom, wife, and professor. She likes to laugh at life's nonsense. In her years before all the current roles she plays, she liked to sail, read, and take long swims along a shoreline. Now she drives people around in her car when she's not busy verbally driving people to get them to clean the house. Writing is an outlet that lets life inside, outside, and all-around sides come together.

Cynthia Schulz is a mom of four young adults, one of whom has disabilities. All have shaped her more than any corner office ever could. After a notable career as a corporate executive, she's embarked on her encore career as an author, speaker, and voice to be reckoned with. Her book of stories—*Shine On, Raising Our Kids with Disabilities to Lead Bright, Happy Lives*—reads like a love letter. Learn more at www.cynthiaschulz.com.

Liz Sheahan has lived in the Midwest and Southern California. Currently, she makes her home in Boise, Idaho, where she works in the nonprofit sector, enjoys her family, her friends, and, of course, her pets, who bring her love, frustration, fear, and immense joy.

Ryma Shohami is a retired technical writer/editor who specialized in documenting business software as well as medical instruments and procedures. She now enjoys devoting much of her time to publishing more nonfiction in several anthologies. Her voice tends toward humor writing, but more serious stories are also in the works.

Mona Smith escaped suburbia for a small farm, where she writes and proudly serves as Head Chicken Wrangler. Her writing has appeared in local newspapers and anthologies, and it would be remiss not to mention her highly praised Christmas letters. Mona loves to try anything once, which usually ends up as a mishap-filled adventure that brings the saying "You can't make this up" vividly to life in her writing.

Dot Suggett is a Bible translator-exegete who spent the better part of twenty-eight years in West Africa with her husband and two daughters. She loves birds, nature, and camping, which pretty much describes her years in rural West Africa. Her dream is to birdwatch, travel, and write at the not-yet-determined time in her retirement. She lives in Ontario, Canada, with her husband, Colin. They do not have any pets.

Maggie van Galen is a lifelong storyteller who believes in following your dreams and signs every book with that reminder. Born and raised in northern Michigan, she studied advertising, journalism, and creative writing at Michigan State University. After a winding path through multiple careers, states, and countries, Maggie found her calling as an author and wordsmith, blending creativity and heart into every story she tells and every word she writes.

Copyright Details

Share Your Funny

Want to see your story in a future edition of a *Burnt Gloveboxes* anthology?

To see our current open submissions, visit ginaramseyauthor.com

Acknowledgments

I extend my sincerest gratitude to everyone who has supported my vision to expand the *Burnt Gloveboxes*® brand into a series, with *Animal Mayhem* as the first anthology.

To my husband, Paul, thank you for being one of my biggest supporters and my personal chef since I began my writing journey. Who am I kidding? You've been creating and plating amazing meals since 1989. This prevented me from withering away; thank goodness. I appreciate your amazing culinary masterpieces, your love, and the support you've provided throughout this entire wild journey we've been on together.

To my amazing kids, Jackie, Mike, and Katie, your love and support have not gone unnoticed. You are all an inspiration to me, and the reason I continue this journey of sharing funny stories with our world.

To my grandson, Merakai, thank you for your appreciation of both animals and humor, and for the combination of the two. Always keep that spark of joy and keep on laughing at all the funny things life brings your way.

To the *Burnt Gloveboxes*® community, I feel honored for the opportunity to feature your tales of animal hijinks in *Animal Mayhem: When Wild Things Go Wilder*. You are all amazing, as are the scenarios you all shared. Tears of joy filled my eyes as I read your stories, as you have all helped me to accomplish this amazing dream of creating the *Burnt Gloveboxes*® anthology.

I would also like to thank all the writers who submitted stories that weren't selected. Writing and submitting a story for consideration requires immense bravery and vulnerability. I want you to know I recognize the hard work and dedication you put into your craft and encourage you to continue writing and sharing your stories. I am incredibly proud of you.

To the *Animal Mayhem* volunteer reader team, thank you to each of you for your time and dedication to the *Animal Mayhem* project. Your feedback was incredibly valuable.

To the *Animal Mayhem* ARC readers, thank you so much for taking the time during the busy holiday season to review these amazing tales of *Animal Mayhem* and for providing your feedback to inform other readers what they are in for.

To Frank Chindamo, thank you for the time you invested in reading *Animal Mayhem* and writing the wonderful foreword. Your knowledge and expertise in the promotion of using humor as a healing tool and creating a positive impact on our world, particularly in the medical community. I salute you, my friend, and I am honored to share a common vision: using laughter as medicine. Thank you for your endorsement of *Animal Mayhem*.

Debby Kevin, there are not enough words to say how much I appreciate you, your skill, and expertise. You are the reason this anthology has come together so smoothly. For this, I will forever be grateful. You saw the possibility and success in my vision and helped to bring it to life. Thank you from the bottom of my heart. To the Highlander Press editing, graphics, and support team, you have been one of the biggest blessings on my author journey.

Another shout-out to Pat Creedon for the amazing cover design. You have captured the essence of *Animal Mayhem* beautifully. Thank you so much.

And finally, to you, reader of *Animal Mayhem* and the other books in the Burnt Gloveboxes® series, I thank you for your support and love. Despite the frequent mishaps, I feel like I am the luckiest gal on this earth.

About Gina Ramsey

Photo credit: JoAnn Jardine

Gina Ramsey is a multifaceted individual with an affection for screaming rubber chickens and a passion for making a difference in the world through humor, inspiration, and connection. Based in the picturesque Superior, WI, she wears many hats: medical social worker, author, entrepreneur, podcast host, and family chaos coordinator.

As an author and humorist, Gina is the guru of "finding the funny" in life's crazy mishaps and blunders popularized in her *Burnt Gloveboxes®* series. Her previous books, *Burnt Gloveboxes: Embracing Life When It Goes Up in Flames, Volumes I and II*, also humorously explore life's unexpected moments.

As a speaker, Gina champions using laughter to improve health and well-being. She cohosts the *Laugh Lines and Turbulence* podcast. She facilitates writer's groups, including Finding the Funny Ink Humor Writers Network, where she connects humor writers with writing, publishing, and marketing professionals.

Gina is a proud mother and grandmother. She and her husband, Paul, are servants to their three cats and miniature dachshund. Learn more by visiting www.ginaramseyauthor.com

facebook.com/ginaramsey429

instagram.com/ginaramsey429

About the Publisher

Highlander Press® is more than a publishing house—we're a movement.

Founded in 2019, Highlander Press® exists to elevate powerful stories that inspire change, spark conversation, and expand what's possible. We specialize in guiding purpose-driven authors—from initial concept to beautifully published book—with clarity, confidence, and unparalleled support.

Our model is intentionally collaborative. We work hand-in-hand with each author to demystify the publishing process, champion creative integrity, and deliver top-tier results without the smoke and mirrors. Every author who walks through our doors is seen, heard, and supported—because we know that behind every great book is a courageous voice ready to rise.

At Highlander Press®, you're not just publishing a book—you're stepping into your next chapter as a leader, a visionary, and a changemaker.

facebook.com/highlanderpress
instagram.com/highlanderpress
tiktok.com/@highlanderpress
linkedin.com/company/highlander-press

Also from Highlander Press®

Anthologies

The Author's Toolkit

Becoming Unstoppable

Heart-Centered Marketing

Your First Year: What I Wish I'd Known

Best-Selling Books

The Divorce Money Map by Donna Jean Kendrick

Unbreakable Us by Joëlle Lydon

Line Magic by Kris Faatz

Shelf Life by Deborah Kevin, MA

Sometimes I Think I Suck by Tal Fagin

In Motion by Joanne Flynn Black

Burnt Gloveboxes (Vol. II) by Gina Ramsey

Free Spirit at Free Safety by Joe Zagorski

Gray Matter by Avery Volz

Fourteen Stones by Kris Faatz

Smooth Sailing (2nd Ed.) by Cheri Andrews, Esq.

Juris Ex Machina by John W. Maly

The Knowing by Kimberly Patton

Thriving Through Cancer by Kelly Lutman

Burnt Gloveboxes (Vol. I) by Gina Ramsey

The Selfish Hour by Megan Weisheipl

Intuitive Languages by Nicole Meltzer

What Color Am I? by Sarah Patterson

Smooth Sailing by Cheri Andrews, Esq.

Peace in Passing (2nd Ed.) by Maribeth Decker

Hang on Tight! by Suzanne Tregenza Moore

A Path of Oneness by Ellen Feldman

Loud Woman by Jill Celeste, MA

By a Thread by Nicolette Blanco

Your4Truths by Judy Kane

You, Me, and Anxiety series by Dr. Robyn Reu Graham

That First Client (2nd Ed.) by Jill Celeste

You've Written Your Book. Now What? by Deborah Kevin

The Gift of Loss by Cathy Agasar

30 *Second Success* by Laura Templeton

Children's Titles

Betty Bartholomew and the Vanishing Begonias by Connie Jo Miller

Sara Smitherson and the Disappearing Snickerdoodles by Connie Jo Miller

Penelope Parsons and the Missing Pomegranates by Connie Jo Miller

My Body Knows. Do I Know? by Ashley Cournoyer-Smith

Meatball and Birdie by Elle Fox

Glitter Bird by Angie Bird

Lauren and Val Take a Walk by Lauren Eileen

Forthcoming Titles

The Five Widows Club by Dr. Tina Fornwald

Eternal Enchantment by Kimberly Patton

Beyond The Jersey by Dr. Justin S. Williams

We'll Be Right Back by Dr. Ann Marie Peters

Voice Lessons by Brandon Wilson

Finding Grace by Deborah Kevin